John Smith

JOHN SMITH

Life and Soul of the Party

GORDON BROWN · JAMES NAUGHTIE

with an introduction by
ELIZABETH SMITH

MAINSTREAM
PUBLISHING
EDINBURGH AND LONDON

First published in Great Britain in 1994 by
MAINSTREAM PUBLISHING COMPANY
(EDINBURGH) LTD
7 Albany Street
Edinburgh EH1 3UG

ISBN 1 85158 692 X

A catalogue record for this book is available from the British Library

Typeset in Sabon by Litho Link Ltd, Welshpool, Wales

Printed in Great Britain by Butler & Tanner Ltd, Frome, Somerset

'There is something fundamental happening in this country now . . . I believe everything is moving our way. We must never be complacent and must never take anything for granted but I believe the signs are set fairer for the Labour Party than they have been for a very long time . . . We will do our best to reward your faith in us but please give us the opportunity to serve our country. That is all we ask.'

With these words John Smith finished the speech he made on the night before he died. This book is dedicated to the Labour Government he did not live to see.

Elizabeth Smith

Contents

Introduction

by

Elizabeth Smith

When John died in May a great many people, most of them unknown to me, wrote to tell me how much he had meant to them. There were letters and cards from all over the country. As they arrived in their hundreds I came to realise the extent to which my husband had carried the hopes of all kinds of people, and at a time of awful loss I was somehow sustained by the discovery that so many other people shared it. Many, many people had looked to John to do things for them and their communities, to represent them and their interests at the highest level, and trusted him and believed he would do it well. His sudden death left them bereft too.

One of the main reasons for putting together this book, and doing so quite quickly, is that it will set on record what kind of person John was, what influences shaped him, what he believed in and how he worked, to let people, like those who were kind enough to write to me in May, know more about him: as politician, as family man, as companion and friend.

I first met John – very traditionally, at a Glasgow University Union dance – in the autumn of 1962. He had already graduated with an MA in history and was studying for his law degree, and was active in student life. He had spoken in the Glasgow University debating team that had won the *Observer* Mace, and was convener of debates. Even then he was committed to a life of politics, and had stood the previous year as a by-election candidate in East Fife.

His debating, like his involvement in student politics, was serious – it was, after all, part of his preparation for later life – but it was also great fun. I was non-political though leftish, and studying modern languages, but soon found myself – thanks to John – in a busy, purposeful world of politics, of ideas, talk and campaigning. There was tremendous energy about, and great humour too; John and his circle worked hard and played hard, and many people from those days became

11

life-long friends, among them Donald Dewar, Jimmy Gordon, Derry Irvine, Donald MacCormick, Neil MacCormick, Ken Munro and Bob McLaughlan.

John finished his law degree and set about the business of becoming a Glasgow solicitor. I went to London to make use of my Russian in a job with the Great Britain-USSR Association, a Foreign Office funded organisation. We kept in touch for several years, making good use of cheap late-night flights – 10 p.m. departure, only two pounds ten shillings – between Glasgow and London, while he completed his training. I had a job, but not what John would have thought a proper job. He took a serious view of such things as professional security, and when I returned to Glasgow it was to teacher training at Jordanhill College and teaching at Glasgow High School for Girls: in John's terms, a proper job.

He sold his car to buy me an engagement ring, but was typically realistic in pointing out that my 'proper job' would bring in enough to help him make the then precarious transition from Glasgow solicitor to Edinburgh advocate. This too at a time when the Edinburgh Bar presented something of the appearance of an exclusive club in which incomers from the West were not very welcome.

He had told me almost as soon as we had met that he was going to be an MP, and as we became closer he never glamorised what it might mean for me. 'I'm offering you a pretty tough life,' he would say. 'It'll be lonely for you, and not much fun.' Then later: 'There'll be tough times to come, but if you can face all that . . . would you like to marry me?'

Our first home was a flat near the foot of Edinburgh's Royal Mile – rented of course, since no one would provide a mortgage for anyone facing the financial uncertainties of an advocate in his first year. Malcolm Rifkind, then also a young advocate, was a neighbour. The Edinburgh Bar proved more welcoming than we had anticipated. John worked hard – he worked hard at everything he took on – and soon found plenty of work to do.

When he stood for a second time in East Fife in 1964 I went campaigning with him. As a previously non-political person I had to learn, but learned quickly, carried along by John's confidence and enthusiasm. He was in his element: assured and natural, a born politician enjoying himself enormously and doing what he had always wanted to do. He did better but didn't win. Then there were the uncertainties of the search for selection for a constituency that might get him to Westminster: some disappointments, and some seats he was lucky not to get.

Meanwhile, there was the law. He enjoyed it, relished court work and grew genuinely to love the life of the Edinburgh Bar. The Bar is very meritocratic: if you're good, you get on. John was, and did. The Bar is also a sociable, comradely little world, small enough to allow people to get to know each other well. John made many friends there – he made friends wherever he went – and kept them.

He was elected to Parliament in 1970 as MP for the old North Lanarkshire constituency. As a backbencher he could still practise law, and it was always important to him to have an alternative to politics, if only to enable him to make his own political judgements without the pressure of having no other career to fall back on. As his political career advanced he stayed in touch, trying to do a few cases each year in the summer recess, until, when he became Shadow Chancellor, it was no longer possible or sensible.

Politics for John was synonymous with Labour politics. Without being at all ideological, he had a deep commitment to the things Labour stands for. He did not agonise at the time when the Right split off to form the SDP. It was the Labour Party that he loved and served and identified with, and it simply never occurred to him to leave it, however much those who did might criticise him for not leaving with them. And if the Labour Party had disintegrated then, he would simply have left politics.

He was a Labour loyalist by instinct, and a pragmatist by inclination. He acknowledged that the Left had a place in the Labour Party, but was utterly unimpressed by what he regarded as its self-indulgence. Real politics – his kind – was in the real world, serving real people.

It was a matter of great pride to him to have served for six months as the youngest minister in Jim Callaghan's Cabinet. He understood office, having had a junior post at Energy and responsibilities for the Devolution Bill, and took to it with zeal. He believed ministers should lead from the front, taking firm charge of their departments, and he had the stamina and application to succeed at it. As a Cabinet minister he worked incredibly hard, and enjoyed it too. But three days after the fall of the Labour Government in 1979 he was back at the Edinburgh Bar.

There followed 15 years in Opposition. Sometimes it was frustrating and sometimes a great test of John's determination, because he was not temperamentally suited to Opposition. He wanted to do things, to change things and to see ideas followed through into practice.

John was not ambitious for himself. He saw politics as service to others, and when Neil Kinnock stood down, he saw leading the Party as just another opportunity to serve. And he remained an intensely practical politician. When he was asked – as all leaders are – what his 'big idea' was, and how he was going to get it across, preferably in three words, his reply was simple: 'A Labour Government.'

Despite all the time and energy John put into the law and politics over the years, his family was immensely important to him. Whatever his commitments, he made a point of being at home in Edinburgh every weekend. Holidays with John were invigorating rather than simply relaxing: he did his best to unwind, sketching and painting, but never succeeded in unwinding sufficiently to master the techniques involved. He preferred doing things that involved setting targets, making lists and ticking them off. Perhaps that was one reason why the idea of climbing nearly 300 Munros came to appeal to him.

Before his first heart attack in 1989 I had never previously worried much about John's health, but in a diary of mine that turned up recently I found little notes over the years, after each successive Labour Conference, saying things like 'John not very well'. He did not particularly enjoy Labour Conferences, though it would have been hard to tell from seeing him there. As always, he worked and played hard, giving the whole thing one hundred per cent from dawn till very late. He came home from the 1989 Conference, the first for years I had not attended with him, and on the Sunday complained – for almost the first time ever – of feeling ill. Being John, he didn't want to bother a doctor, but a doctor neighbour – who later became one of his first mountaineering companions – was called and sent John straight in to the Royal Infirmary.

In Casualty they did a cardiography, assured him it was normal ('Whatever it is, it's not your heart') but as he was putting his shoes on he went, in his own words, 'into the dark'. Prompt and skilled action by Infirmary cardiologists saved his life. The next three months he spent at home: reading, thinking and gradually rebuilding his fitness.

As with everything else he did, his commitment was total. He read everything there was to read about getting over a heart attack and mastered the science of dieting. One of my daughters even complained she couldn't open the fridge without getting a brisk lesson on the precise caloric value of whatever she was thinking of snacking on. He lost weight, got fit and at last discovered the perfect form of relaxation.

We had walked and rambled as a family for years, sometimes in a big informal group, the Radical Ramblers, consisting of university friends, political colleagues and their families, but as John recovered from his heart attack he began to climb seriously. The Munros – Scottish mountains over 3,000 feet – became the new challenge. There are 277 of them, a series of targets, some of them very, very demanding: a list to check, the perfect relaxation for him.

He climbed well over a hundred, many with Murray Elder, who later in this book introduces excerpts from their Munro diary. It was fun and a challenge, and a way of showing himself and the world that after his heart attack he had not only recovered but made himself far fitter than before.

John died at the height of his political powers and in a job he loved – that of Leader of the Labour Party. He did not live to see again his 'big idea': a Labour Government, but in the outpouring of grief and sympathy that followed his death it was clear that millions of people had taken it for granted that he would lead one. Most of the tributes, public and private, seemed to say the same thing: that John Smith had been expected to realise in Government the principle he had held for years, that his sense of fairness, his instinct for social justice and economic efficiency, reflected the aspirations of millions of ordinary people. He was their champion, and his life had been cut short on the brink of his, and their, hour of fulfilment.

I was glad recently to come across an article John wrote, *I Love Islands*, for although as a pragmatist he accepted that the pursuit of a career at the Scottish Bar meant living in Edinburgh and the life of a politician meant spending a great deal of time in London, he never lost his love of Argyll, where he was born. It is perhaps fitting that at the end of that article he sings the praises of Iona, where we spent so many happy holidays and where he is now buried.

This book sets out to tell people about John: as a family man, a lawyer and politician. In this foreword, and in a section by Sarah, my oldest daughter, the family view of John uses family sources. James Naughtie, an experienced political commentator, sets John's political life in its context. Gordon Brown, a friend and close political associate for years, contributes a section on John's political thinking as reflected in his public statements. In various ways Donald Dewar, Jimmy Gordon and Colin Currie also helped.

I am grateful to them, and to Bill Campbell of Mainstream, for making this book possible and also producing it so quickly. It is dedicated to John's memory. I hope it will serve also to reach out to the many people who reached out so kindly to me at the time of his death.

Edinburgh
August 1994

Part One

John Smith:
Politics and Philosophy

Tribute

by

Donald Dewar

At Cluny Church, Edinburgh, on 19 May, Donald Dewar paid tribute to his late friend.

A journalist talking to me recently chose to decry John's consistency as though it were a fault.

He was indeed a man consistent of purpose but this was a strength. His principles lasted throughout his life.

At a time of loss, you remember and remember. The other day someone produced the GU Handbook of 1959. In it John, aged 21, writing on behalf of the Labour Club, proclaimed that 'in this Club we think it valuable occasionally to indulge in political activities such as canvassing.'

Even in my post Presbyterian moments I would not describe canvassing as an indulgence – a penance perhaps, never an indulgence. Given his work rate then and through the years it must have been a case of breaking the bad news gently.

More importantly, in that article John set out what he described as his 'credo'.

He believed that 'the opportunity of each individual to lead a complete and civilised life should be equal as far as possible to that of his neighbour' and there followed a plea for a more just distribution of material wealth.

He laid out then principles which he argued right to the end.

He would often tell me of individual problems he came across in the constituency or on the stump – cases where the system presses sorely on families already struggling to cope with hard times. John's anger and frustration was something you could almost touch.

He knew that poverty and inequality killed life chances: that for too many failure became a self-fulfilling prophecy.

John was not interested in the trappings of power. He wanted power

19

not for what it did for him, but for what it might allow him to do for others.

There were great causes straddling the years for which, whatever the price, he stood his ground. He was consistent.

I remember John working his guts out in student days to elect Albert Luthuli Rector of the University at a time when the horror of apartheid was not a universal student cause. We elected Luthuli who then symbolised the struggle in South Africa and could not take office as Rector because of prison bars.

I remember John's joy when Mandela was freed and freely elected. I do not object to such consistency of principle and purpose.

There was the need for a positive and constructive approach to Europe, which led John to defy the Whips as a young backbencher – just one example of the courage that marked and made his career.

There was his determination that power should not be a monopoly hoarded in Whitehall and Westminster. It was a principle relevant to every part of this kingdom, but with a special significance for Scotland and for John who made his Parliamentary reputation fighting the Scotland Act onto the Statute Book in 1978. It was this unfinished business to which he intended to return.

There will be many – some here today – who thought he was wrong in these views, but who could deny the sincerity, the tenacity and the true spirit of the man.

Consistency was at the core of him. Politics a series of practical problems to be overcome. Square, determined, sometimes thrawn, always probing, pushing for a way forward.

His life and his work, his reassuring presence, were a standing reproach to the easy cynicism that brands politics as a dishonest game.

He was, of course, consistent in friendship. Politicians of real stature gather around them friends who are prepared to fight for them even when they are in error. John had that ability. He did not command, he earned respect. I was proud to be one of his friends.

I will remember the good times. Those who saw John as douce, dark suited and safe knew not the man.

He could start a party in an empty room – and often did – filling it with good cheer, Gaelic songs and argument.

He enjoyed people and loyalty was a prime virtue, and never with John a one-way process.

He would walk through walls to help a friend – I can bear witness to that.

John was always himself. He was genuine through and through.

He told the truth.

What has been striking over the last dark week has not been the tributes of the great and the good – handsome as they have been – but the sadness, the dismay, the sense of loss across the range of our community. The people have lost a friend – someone who was on their side and they know it.

20

A Political Life Observed

by

James Naughtie

A Leader of the Opposition who never becomes Prime Minister is bound to be something of a puzzle, because the most important questions are never answered. A Leader of the Opposition who never has the chance to fail to become Prime Minister in a general election is more enigmatic still, because voters have never been able to pass judgement on what they have seen so far. That career will always have a mysterious side to it.

No-one can know how it would have ended if it had run its course and been crowned by victory or defeat, and no-one can know whether the sentiments of the political campaigner in Opposition would have sustained a premiership. John Smith's fate, shared by so many who have plied his trade, is that the judgement of his worth may eventually be decided not by what he did, but simply by what happens next.

If Labour win the next general election he will be guaranteed a certain heroic status. With Neil Kinnock he will enter history as a builder of foundations, and his strengths rather than his weaknesses will be remembered. Without him, it will be said by nearly everybody in that new Government, it could never have happened. But defeat? Another lost election after 17 or 18 years of Conservative Government and the story of the early Nineties will be lost in the storm of argument. Nobody can predict its course, except that it would be confused and confusing, with talk of betrayal and plenty of sectarian bickering, and that much of a generation in the party would quietly slip off to grow old in a place away from the sun. In that kind of world there wouldn't be much room for the brief leadership that was the bridge between Neil Kinnock and Tony Blair.

So the Smith years are in the balance. His own practical politician's sense would make him wonder if a leadership spent entirely in Opposition could ever be a real success. But it would also persuade him that it couldn't be said to be a failure if, as he believed, he had done

21

things for his party which not only would help it win power after the barren years but which were also irreversible, and were therefore a legacy that couldn't easily be squandered.

The question for his parliamentary colleagues and his party at large is easy. Did he bring Government closer? They will get their answer – one they will have to accept, be it good or ill – before long. For outsiders trying to find where his preliminary place in history might lie, it's more complicated because it involves trying to look at him without being dazzled by the one issue that interests the shadow cabinet above all – whether their careers will lead them at last into ministerial office.

And it means, too, not being dazzled by the way his career ended. Because his death was a shock, and because he was so self-evidently a good and decent man even to those who hardly knew him and had only a hazy image in their minds, something of a national convulsion occurred when he'd gone. The question is how much it had to do with what he represented and had achieved. In the talk of principles and values that became the fashion and helped to shape the Labour leadership election, was there a real legacy? After all, tragedies in public life always encourage melodramatic reactions. That is their nature. Some of the things said just after his death would have made him roar with laughter in his characteristic way, slapping his thighs with both hands and doubling himself up with mirth. He'd especially have enjoyed the contortions of some newspapers which had been writing him off and suddenly began to write of him as a kind of lost champion, plucked from the world as his moment of triumph approached.

So the mists swirl across the 22 months he led his party. Through them some see a man preparing himself in a model way for office, taking his time in the way of confident people who know what will happen next. There are others who see a leader with the great strength of a natural caution which kept him from making too many mistakes, but who was in danger of giving too much attention to the long game at the expense of the here and now. That was the view of some close colleagues.

These are political calculations of the moment, about how a policy was managed or a majority squeezed out of a reluctant conference, or how a new strategy was devised. Real substance in politics involves something else, a sense that leadership comes naturally. And leaders aren't simply the people who win more votes than their rivals, though from time to time they must. They are the ones who can learn as they go without losing their originality or their authority. Donald Dewar, Smith's friend for more than 35 years, said at his funeral that it was characteristic of the big figures in politics that they had around them people whose loyalty they had won and could hold, and who would follow when the call came. Smith certainly had a band of brothers round him who would take their lead from him and support him in troubled times, knowing that the help would be returned when it was needed.

From that he gained considerable political strength. Tactical battles are easier to win if you have loyal cohorts who have committed themselves to you and have decided that their political careers and yours are bound up together and aren't worth much if they are pulled apart.

That loyalty sprang principally from Smith's personality and not his position. Being naturally gregarious he was a lucky collector of friends, and he was never a questioner of the value of friendship: it was as much the stuff of politics to him as the late-night manoeuvre along the committee corridor in the Commons or at a party conference, the jab of the verbal stiletto at the turning point of a long meeting. And the love of companionship for its own sake was buttressed by an instinctive sense of obligation to friends and colleagues. It didn't mean that there shouldn't be rough stuff in pursuit of a political objective; it did mean that loyalty to those who supported him was something he was determined not to compromise.

The trick of politics is in finding a way of letting such personal commitments and the demands of power live happily together. No-one doubts Smith's values – an undoctrinaire Christianity, a sharp sense of social justice, a common humanity – and no-one looking at his career can miss the political successes, though there were failures too. Yet it is not easy yet to say exactly what it amounted to. Was his leadership potent enough to win the election? Was there really a strong Prime Minister inside him waiting to jump out, as so many claimed? Was the celebration of a moral approach to politics after his death prompted more by that tragedy than a mood he had created in life? In short, how effectively had Smith turned his convictions into a political style and method of leadership that could win over the electorate and succeed in Government?

Judging Smith means searching for him first. More than many men and women at the top of politics in recent times he was obviously moulded by his background and by consistent beliefs through the years. His tactics in the Leader of the Opposition's office under Big Ben weren't skills learned late in the day. They were as much a reflection of his personality and his attitudes as any speech he ever made on the morality of politics. In that sense this politician who is a puzzle because he was struck down too soon is no puzzle at all. He is an open book.

So this is a glance at its pages. It's no biography – historians will take care of that in their time – only a few fragments which make an impressionistic picture of a politician through the life he led and the times he lived in. And the place to start is Scotland because it explains so much.

A DEMOCRATIC INTELLECT

It seemed strange to John Smith and to many of his companions that he was usually described as an Edinburgh lawyer, as if that was a category so well-defined as to say everything. In the way that a craggy, calloused Northern Labour MP in the old days might be called a Yorkshire miner and it was left at that, the label was assumed to speak for itself. But it was misleading.

Smith lived in Edinburgh and he practised law. In a city full of lawyers, which also has a dubious reputation as a place where the professional classes live behind spectacular social battlements, that seemed to outsiders to be the background you needed to know. The opposite was true. It was a backcloth that needed to be lifted to see what lay behind.

All his life Smith felt himself to be a West of Scotland man. All the nonsense about old divisions having disappeared in Scotland, and Glasgow and Edinburgh having learned to live together, should be forgotten. Culturally, you carry your territory with you through life: there are assumptions about coming from East or West which still colour Scottish life, and not always for the worse. Anyone outside Scotland who still doubts that two cities less than an hour apart by train can still feel like this should study the recent history of the argument – explosion, really – about the siting of a new National Gallery of Scottish Art. They fought like a couple of ancient city-states dividing the spoils of war and protecting their political *amour propre*. And those who tried to impose some lofty commonsense from outside found it a hard job.

Behind such public displays of tribal loyalty to a city-state is something more substantial. Scotland's size has meant that individuality has been preserved: everyone knows where everyone else comes from, so everyone has a past. In professional Scotland the four ancient universities, all founded by the early 17th century, have kept their sway. And Smith was a Glasgow man. Not only does that mark you out in a public way, it becomes a way of identifying yourself. Scots of John Smith's sort talk about their backgrounds and their education with a certain simple pride and (mostly) without the preciousness too often associated with Oxbridge, though it would be a blind man who ignored the steamy rivalries between the fee-paying schools in both Glasgow and Edinburgh which yield to none in their capacity for fighting tired old social battles.

Living in Edinburgh was one thing, coming from the West another. The traditional assumption, not always justified, is that the Glasgow man has a down-to-earth commonsense that contrasts with the more effete Edinburgh middle-class manners. Caricatures of course, very crude ones, but built into the humour and the social habits of the cities still.

In a way, Smith felt himself to be a graduate of Glasgow University as much as anything else he ever was. To those who haven't gone through one of the old Scottish universities – at least as they were in the Fifties – this must seem odd. But it was the place where he found his style. And law students in those days had an advantage. The old system meant that before you read law you often had to finish an arts degree first. When you emerged you would be MA LLB, the letters Scottish lawyers still like to have after their names. So Smith read history before he started on the law, and began learning with all his colleagues how Scots law had developed from the Roman code in a quite separate way from the English common law tradition. This was a broad education, which also had the advantage of making law students feel rather special. They would be practising in a small, well-ordered world. There were fewer than a hundred advocates – Scottish barristers – when Smith graduated, though no-one will be surprised to know that they have multiplied their numbers happily in recent years. Moreover, they felt that they were defenders of a particular tradition.

There are plenty of examples of failings in the Scottish legal system and the boasts made on its behalf have often involved more bravado than fact, but it has nonetheless preserved a distinct character. Despite the cosiness and complacency that naturally follows from that, students in Smith's day could feel a kind of pride in its difference. It had – the most difficult word in Scotland – independence.

And university life in Glasgow in the late Fifties was rather more relaxed than it was to become in later years. Law students knew they would get work, and that they would probably make a good living to keep them for the rest of their days. And life on what no-one would ever have called the campus was lively, despite the apparently inhibiting fact that in Glasgow a large proportion of the students lived at home. The political clubs were big and their rivalries somehow tamer than the sectarian battles on Left and Right that would dominate the scene for later generations of students.

Smith's natural home was the Labour Club, and you can see in it the seeds of the later career. It was loyalist, in the sense that it was passionate for Hugh Gaitskell, then fighting against the Bevanite Left. In a later period of Labour history the tilt in universities would be quite the other way. Of course the students of that time had not had a recent Labour Government to complain about – none of the 'betrayals' laid at the door of Wilson and Callaghan which were the stuff of dissent – but it also seemed natural to them, as characters who could look forward to prosperous careers in the law or in politics in the Labour establishment in Scotland, that this was the place to be. Not for Smith the pleasures of minority politics, fighting the system.

It was a lively gang. Smith was followed as Chairman of the Labour Club by Donald MacCormick, the broadcaster, and Donald Dewar, later his shadow cabinet colleague. With them were characters like Alexander 'Derry' Irvine, later to become a leading QC in England, now a peer and a possible future Labour Lord Chancellor, whose chambers, incidentally, were the training ground for a young Tony Blair. In the milieu that encompassed the political clubs and the Union debating society were figures like Teddy Taylor, later a feisty political opponent for Smith, and Menzies Campbell, who also became a QC before being elected as a

Liberal Democrat MP. There was Jimmy Gordon, who founded Radio Clyde and became a power in the land, and Neil MacCormick – Donald's cousin – later to become a distinguished academic lawyer but then known in Glasgow (with his brother Iain, later an SNP MP) as the offspring of John MacCormick, the man who had been the inspiration for the Nationalist surge after the war years and the power behind the extraordinary Scottish Covenant movement which sought to stir a rather dozy populace to the idea of independence. It failed, in the sense that it was not until the mid-Seventies that nationalism won a significant parliamentary voice, but it was part of the political landscape that Smith and his colleagues knew intimately. This was a world where there was quite a bit of romance in politics.

Such feelings certainly did not flow from most of the Labour MPs of that era. They were generally grey. Political machines gripped many constituencies – and in the West of Scotland, religious sectarianism was an often unspoken but pervasive influence on politics. Of course there were honourable exceptions in Parliament, but you didn't look to the Scottish group of Labour MPs for much dash and flair in those days. Yet the Fifties were ending, and perhaps the first glimmerings of the passing of an old order were on the horizon. For young Labour students, the Macmillan Government and its patrician Scottish outposts were happy targets.

Not that these political days were particularly serious. Anyone tempted to think so should remember Dewar's election campaign in the Labour Club, and compare it with the upright image he carries today (one which underplays his great wit). His slogan, John Smith used to enjoy claiming afterwards, had been 'Vote Dewar X – and be safe'. A pun before its time, you might say. The atmosphere was quite uproarious. Smith and his colleagues enjoyed themselves. He and Dewar trod the debating circuit, winning prizes and having fun, and prepared, inevitably, for real politics.

That would come in the bitter struggles in the Glasgow Labour Party in the early Sixties when the sluggish old machine was being challenged by the Left. There was manipulation everywhere, rough organisational battles and many accusations of malpractice. Smith was in the thick of it. By this stage he'd established his own beliefs – in the terms of those days he was firmly on the Right – and his style. And in Glasgow it has never been forgotten. To this day the opponents in those early struggles still exchange accusations. Some wounds have never healed. The point is that these days saw Smith as he would be half a lifetime later. Two strands are intertwined, a certain kind of education with its particular expectations, and a set of political beliefs and a style. This is a story of politics set firmly in Scotland, shaped by its history and contemporary social conventions. The world that John Smith inhabited was able to make him one of its own, and this is the beginning of the explanation of that conjunction in him which continues to puzzle outsiders even after his death. He was seen to be an establishment figure in many ways, besuited and sober in manner. That Edinburgh lawyer. Yet he spoke about the redistribution of wealth, about the importance of social justice, with the language of a radical reformer – arguing, for example, for tax plans which were more openly redistributive than the ones advocated by some colleagues who were generally placed to his left. How, they asked, could a Gaitskellite who worked with the old political machine in the West of Scotland in the Sixties be something else too. In a Scottish setting the explanation is easy.

Glasgow University was invigorating for him, but there was something else too. John Smith grew up in a village schoolhouse in Ardrishaig in Argyll, a quite remote and beautiful place. Most towns, let alone any cities, were a long way away. He imbibed in those days the essence of a tradition which still permeates Scottish life, though it flows much less strongly than it once did: education is important, maybe the most important thing of all. It would be taken for granted in the Smith house that books were good, that learning had its own reward, that self-improvement was the thing. Mostly, the idea has been devoid of the dafter effusions of homespun philosophers of the Samuel Smiles school in the 19th century because it had at its heart another principle which was egalitarian.

Since the Reformation in the 16th century when Scotland began its religious and social revolution, John Knox's phrase 'a school in every parish' has been passed down through the generations. The passage was hardly smooth, of course, and anyone who pretends that Scotland has progressed down some happy winding road of social progress for all, with education as its guiding light, is in danger of disappearing into the same enveloping fog as the romantics who celebrate the most peculiar events of Scottish history as if they are the story itself, and not its misleading adornments. Yet education – more accurately, the idea of education – has been a talisman to which Scots have clung as a way of identifying themselves.

Many children of recent generations have been raised on stories of their antecedents setting off for a term at the university with a bag of meal on their back for sustenance. The picture of the 'lad o' pairts' – the youngster who makes good in the world by using all his wits and displaying all his talents – is an image lovingly tended, and passed on. Many did not lead a life like that, of course. And the idea that lay behind it – opportunity for all – often turned out to be a myth. But the idea kept its power. Particularly in rural Scotland the progress through school into the world, or to university, had a special place in the mind of the community. It was a kind of guarantee that here was something available to all. Much of Scotland still retains its feudal instinct – wild talk about Scotland being classless is nonsensical – but in its institutions it has continued to pay obeisance to the ideal of egalitarianism, a certain spirit of equality. You can't talk about such concepts without a dangerous collision with real experience, but you can point to the way it has shaped the thinking of generations.

There is a phrase that catches it, 'the democratic intellect'. In a famous book on the Scottish universities by that name, George Davie sought to define the egalitarian sense in education in a society that often seemed not to be egalitarian in its habits at all. It springs really from the 18th century when the thinking of the Enlightenment, allied to the huge social changes that had recast Scotland since the Reformation, established the idea of an élite which had nothing to do with birth or inherited power but which reflected the community at large. Hence it was the idea that brought such a mix of students to universities in the 19th century, and gave them for the rest of their lives a natural belief that that was the way things should be.

It's important to realise that this undercurrent flows through all the political parties in Scotland. However great the ideological differences there are some shared beliefs which are thought to be the ones that give Scotland its distinctiveness. Even when they seem to have disappeared, people want to cling to them. No-one should confuse this with political nationalism, which is only one manifestation of it. Widely, across Scottish society there is a sense of educational tradition which persists even when contemporary experience seems to deny that it is still there.

So at the schoolhouse in Ardrishaig young Smith would feel that history instinctively. And in the village where his father was 'dominie' – literally, the master – the traditional twin pillar of the community, with the minister, he drank from that well. The educational institutions of Scotland were important to him, and so were the two others that have given Scots a means beyond politics of holding on to their distinctiveness, through many storms – the law and the church.

The law was another way in which Scotland could feel different. You will not find many fervent Nationalists in Advocates Hall on the Royal Mile in Edinburgh who want political independence, but you will find most of them fervent defenders of a system which defines their country and its traditions for them. The legal hierarchy looks out on the cobbled streets from the building where the Scottish Parliament voted for Union in 1707 – with the Senators of the College of Justice perpetuating the old majesty of Scots law – and it knows it is different. It is a feeling that pleases them. Cynics can point to the convenience of having a small, separate system that provides places on the bench for a goodly number as the years go by, and the joys of living in a close professional community – and they are right to be sceptical about some of the claims made for the differences that exist between the Scots lawyer and his counterparts south of the Tweed. But differences there are.

That distinctiveness is buttressed by the church. Despite the same drift away from formal religious practice in Scotland as elsewhere, the Church of Scotland itself – the Kirk – has managed to keep a position of some strength. Smith grew up in it and, especially in his last years, he found it a helpful companion. Again this produced a kind of mystification outside Scotland because of the confused way in which religion is often described. You'd think sometimes that there was only one faith 'up there', a fire-breathing Calvinism that preaches social conservatism and a puritanical lifestyle. No.

Despite its 19th-century excesses in that direction, and the natural conservative instincts of a national church – national rather than established, the Kirk having no formal state link – its history has stressed the importance of presbyterian government (not a bishop to be seen) and the sense of individual religious belief and practice as the point of the exercise. In that sense, the Kirk is not authoritarian – ministers, after all, are appointed and can be removed by their congregations, though in reality that is the theory rather than the practice. And to use the word 'democratic' about the Kirk would be rather misleading since its institutions, though democratic in form, have tended to be upholders of convention. Yet there is something of the old spirit left.

At its best, and there are plenty examples of it at its worst, the Kirk is engaged in talking about the real world more than in theological hair-splitting. The principal committee at the General Assembly, the parliament of the church, is called the Church and Nation, reminding everybody that if it is not involved in society it is almost as if it does not exist. Now there are disputatious factions in the Kirk, as in any church, and there are dark periods in its past – but like the educational tradition and the law it has preserved enough of its old character, and enough public loyalty, to be one of the ways in which a good number of Scots are happy to help define themselves, by celebrating differences.

As with so many others, John Smith was shaped by these institutions and the social attitudes they preserved. The common ground they all shared was an independence of spirit, and especially in education a championing of the individual. But despite the tales that all Scots children heard, of explorers and inventors and engineers and traders who travelled the world, the idea of community was never lost. A sense of obligation beyond yourself was part of the idea, and it has survived surprisingly well. Remnants of these old assumptions will still be around when this century turns into the next. Not all Scots will be influenced by them – many never have been – but they will still hover around them.

Understanding that background is to understand how a traditionalist style and a feeling for radicalism can coexist. In Scotland the radical tradition was passed on in many homes. In Labour territory it was the story of Red Clydeside, in the Highlands the story of struggles over land. Smith was a Highlander in one sense – Argyll's history is in part the history of Highland feuds – and he sang Gaelic songs in the village school, and later when he travelled down to Dunoon to secondary school, but he was not a native speaker and the heart of Celtic Scotland is further north. Yet there was always something of the Highlander in him, because he had come to Glasgow from what seemed a distant place, where old ways held sway. In later years he and his family spent summers on the Isle of Mull and then on Iona, not too far from Ardrishaig as the crow flies, and it was a natural reflection of his own instincts.

In Scotland it is quite easy to retain something of that sense of being an outsider and to be on the inside. In the small professional world of Edinburgh – like Glasgow – where everyone knows everyone else's business and their personal histories, and paths cross daily as they would in a busy village street, there is inevitably a mingling of backgrounds and attitudes which doesn't seem unnatural at all. It is certainly quite cosy, and easy from outside to be critical of the self-support system it has created for itself, but the point is that it should not be surprising to find someone like John Smith, representing an industrial Lanarkshire seat and feeling comfortable with trade union leaders (as he always had), who would have in his home a *galère* that included judges, bankers, businessmen, academics and people in the arts as well as political colleagues and old friends from other parties. It said nothing about him except the most important thing: the same background that had made him had also made them and it was something they enjoyed celebrating.

By the time he was deep in politics, getting a safe seat after a trial run in East Fife (won many years later for Liberal Democrats by his friend Ming Campbell), that background of the traditional Scots village boy made good had imprinted itself on him. It was therefore appropriate, as well has hugely enjoyable for him, that the first part of his political career came to a climax in a series of events that made Scotland examine itself again, and provided years of mystification and sometimes alarm for the rest of Britain. These were the devolution years, and the years of Smith's rise to fame.

HOME RULE?

In the post-war parliamentary history of Britain there has been nothing quite like the struggle over devolution, which began as an argument that almost no-one outside Scotland understood, split both the main parties at the same time, led the Commons for the first time to vote for the establishment of a Parliament outside London and brought a Government tumbling down.

Looking back from the Nineties it seems now a time of strange excitement which somehow diverted everyone's minds from the day-to-day matters of the economy. That is something of an illusion of course, because the truth is that for many people – not a few in Scotland – the whole episode was a bore. Nonetheless, these were years when a great constitutional change seemed to beckon, when a generation of young Scots politicians began to imagine happy careers in a parliament at home, and when many Nationalists expected embassies to start setting up for business in Edinburgh at any time. It was therefore an affair which seemed to tap the idealism which lay under the surface in Scotland, or at least to revive properly the political argument which had ebbed and flowed through the establishment there for two and a half centuries; but it was also a desperate political manoeuvre.

The Callaghan Government did not embrace devolution because it wanted to, but because it had to. The SNP's successes in the two general elections of 1974 – winning first seven and then 11 seats – and afterwards the loss of four MPs, including two maverick defectors in Scotland on the Home Rule issue, meant that against his instincts the Prime Minister had to press on with a Bill, first of all dealing jointly with Scotland and Wales. It was a predictable disaster, the Bills were separated and rewritten as a result and after two years of bizarre parliamentary capers they were lost as a consequence of two referendums, though of those who voted in Scotland a majority had said Yes.

They were melodramatic years and Smith found himself at the centre of the stage, though often uncomfortably. The episode would establish a parliamentary reputation for him – Michael Foot, under whom he served as a minister, claimed to see a leader in him even then – but it also marked a change in him and his party which was to play an important part in the political convulsions of the Eighties. The background is important because it shows how much changed, and how quickly.

Smith never pretended that his selection for North Lanarkshire to fight the 1970 election was anything other than a traditional Labour fix. He had made a considerable reputation in the party and was obviously clever and personable, so at the retirement of the popular and formidable Peggy Herbison, the local machine – run smoothly in those days by Dick Stewart as agent – chose Smith. And it was not long after his election that he started to shine, eventually becoming Parliament Private Secretary to the Scottish Secretary, Willie Ross, after Labour's return to power by a hairsbreadth in 1974. So the ambitious young lawyer found himself alongside the gruff teacher in Ross, who was a rock-like manifestation of conservative traditional Scottish values and, simultaneously, someone whose passion was the fight against the Nationalists and the narrowness that he thought they represented.

Since Labour's humiliation at the hands of the SNP in the Hamilton by-election of 1967 the embittered feelings between the parties in Labour's traditional areas had become very raw. Ross threw himself into the fight against separation, by which he meant any devolutionary arrangement that might encourage thoughts of independence, and spoke of such things as he might talk of a Satanic ritual. But powerful elements in the Scottish party were demanding that Keir Hardie's old demand for a Scottish Parliament should be exhumed, and they got their way in the end. Deeply conservative elements in the party who saw constitutional change as dangerous were allied with some on the Left who saw appeasement of the SNP as a surrender to narrow nationalism, and a long period of intra-party struggle began.

It was during this time that some of the Labour MPs who now dominate the Scottish group in Parliament were cutting their teeth in the

31

argument with the SNP, and the years that lay ahead were to mark everyone who lived through it. Robin Cook (elected in 1974), sceptic, Gordon Brown, the voice of the pro-devolution Left, Brian Wilson the radical journalist campaigning against the SNP and devolution – they were typical of the ferment of the time. For the first time in their political lives a serious constitutional issue was being argued out in the streets, and moreover it was one which seemed likely to produce change. This was no academic debate; it was about a new parliament.

And Smith found himself put at what may seem now to have been a tangent to the argument, but was in those days the heart of it. The SNP had ridden the tide of oil. It seemed that the North Sea might remove the traditional financial objections to independence by providing an endless stream of money through the pipelines to Shetland, Orkney and Aberdeenshire. 'It's Scotland's Oil' was the cry. For the Labour Government, deeply sensitive to its precarious parliamentary position and the emotive campaigning of the SNP, the North Sea held political dangers as well as the promise of economic growth. Harold Wilson, as Prime Minister, decided that Smith should be the minister for North Sea oil under Tony Benn, the Energy Secretary.

It was an unlikely pairing since even then their differences – especially over Europe and public ownership – were obvious and deep. Yet Smith had no difficulty in carrying through the legislation to establish the public stake in the North Sea. That was not for him a matter between Left and Right but a straightforward matter of protecting the public interest. So the British National Oil Corporation was set up.

The Labour Government at that time was a rickety affair, split over Europe, split over Scotland and seeing the first serious signs on the national executive committee of the strains that would hasten the end of the Callaghan Government and wreak such consequences in the early Eighties. Smith's position in the argument was clear. He hadn't changed since his early days in the party. When Wilson resigned with famous abruptness in 1976, Smith was in the Callaghan camp straight away, arguing the pragmatic case. He didn't have to think long about Roy Jenkins' campaign, despite having been a fellow rebel on Europe five years earlier, defying a three-line Labour whip to support Edward Heath on entry to the Community. Callaghan was more his type of leader, with a love of the greasy levers of power.

Life in Government then was a nervy business. Not only was the Labour Party arguing internally about an economic strategy that would produce something better than Wilson had managed in 1974–76, an argument which would become embarrassingly public and destructive of the Government's cohesion in the IMF crisis only a few months after Callaghan's election as Leader, but the parliamentary numbers were alarming. Technically it was a minority Government. The Nationalists were troublesome, and although Margaret Thatcher was making a slow start as

Leader of the Opposition and hadn't yet found an effective parliamentary style the ground was promising for the Tories. It was in that difficult state that Callaghan found himself proposing radical constitutional change, something which did not seem to come naturally to him.

It certainly did not come naturally to much of his party. Though they had known it was coming – a special conference in Glasgow in 1974 had committed them to it – many Scots MPs were irritated by it. There were the upfront critics – Tam Dalyell, Robin Cook and Bob Hughes among the notables – but there were many more who would stay quiet because they had been schooled in loyalty but who had varying degrees of contempt for the whole business. But Willie Ross was off to the Lords. Bruce Millan as Scottish Secretary was willing to see the commitment through and Michael Foot, as Leader of the Commons, was given Smith as his deputy to get the Bill passed. Time has softened the focus of those years. It was rough. A Labour Government seemed to be running scared of the SNP. Quite a number of ministers were firmly against the policy. It was known that many Labour backbenchers would rebel, because particularly in North-East England there was a feeling of betrayal, that Scotland was getting a special deal. Enthusiasm for devolution in the Labour Party at large was hard to find.

In the next two years an argument swam round the Commons which, looking back, played some part in securing Labour's conversion to constitutional change in the Eighties, from a traditionalist resistance to such innovations – often represented by Roy Hattersley – to a much more flexible approach, championed by Kinnock and carried on by Smith. Blair's Labour Party is still being shaped by that change.

At the time, of course, the Government felt not so much as if it was bent on an idealistic crusade to bring a new kind of government to Scotland (and Wales, though there was no real evidence that Wales ever wanted it) as it was feeling the rod of political necessity on its back. Parliamentary survival was never secure, and in Scotland there was the threat that the SNP would run amok through sleepy Labour territory if the promise of devolution was dropped. Poll after poll said that up to two-thirds of the population wanted a devolved Parliament (and a strong majority opposed independence).

Many English MPs could hardly believe it, but they were in constituencies where no-one had ever had to cope with the kind of panic the SNP had produced in the West of Scotland. The Nationalists' breakthrough had come mainly in rural Scotland at the expense of the Tories, rather paradoxically since the bulk of their members were in industrial seats. But the real target was Labour and a devolution 'betrayal' was all they needed to write their campaign banners.

Devolution was important for Labour, and important for Smith. Apart from the obvious shine it put on his parliamentary reputation – for months on end he was a fixture at the despatch box – it seemed to change his outlook. He argued subsequently that he had always believed in devolution in principle. But there were times – notably when he spoke to the Glasgow special conference in 1974 – when he argued a practical case against legislation now. It can certainly be said that he had a conservative instinct on the question, and probably not just because he was at the side of Ross, who represented traditionalist Labour thinking in its most implacable form.

Smith's colleagues from that time argue that too much is made of his practical scepticism. Whatever the truth of his balance of feeling the episode touches on the way that his background and his political career are connected. The sense of Scottishness that people like Smith felt did not in the Sixties and early Seventies lead them to argue for some form of 'home rule' in the old Liberal sense. The ties to the established Labour ways were too strong and nothing which threatened to dismantle them by creating a new Scottish Parliament and power centre seemed to make sense. It was a threat. Particularly when the SNP started to grow as a result of the defection of Labour voters, the loyalist attitude tended to strengthen.

Smith's commitment to things Scottish, and to the sense of cultural separateness with which he had grown up, was not seen as something that had political implications. Indeed, such thoughts were dangerous because they would play into the hands of Nationalists who were, in the favourite dismissive phrase after their victories of 1974, the 'Tartan Tories'.

The Devolution Bills, though they failed, changed all that in the Labour Party. By the end of the long parliamentary road Smith himself had a real conviction about the Assembly that was to be set up, and an awareness of the excitement it might bring. He never wavered in his commitment afterwards. Indeed it took only a few years after the election defeat of 1979 for the party to commit itself with almost no reservation to a Scottish Parliament and by the mid-Eighties one of the annual tasks of the secretary of the Scottish party was to check carefully beforehand that in the leader's speech at the Scottish conference there was an unambiguous pledge to establish an elected assembly. Kinnock, everyone remembered, had once been a deeply convinced anti-devolutionist.

The process was therefore a turning point though it seemed at the time to reach a dead end. The conviction of some ministers did remain thin throughout. Foot himself appeared not to be convinced by the details of his Bills – characteristically, he tended to ignore the small print – and the whole scheme sat oddly with his concept of parliamentary sovereignty. Others in the Cabinet were scathing. And on the backbenches, especially among the Geordies and those Welsh MPs who felt a Scottish scheme had been thrust unwanted on them (as indeed it had been), there was considerable bitterness which drained support from the Government when it was most needed in the dying days.

Through all this Smith had to keep the Government going in the Commons. It was a marathon. After the Scotland and Wales Bill fell in

1977 when the Commons refused to support a timetable motion – a guillotine – the focus was the Scotland Bill itself, which sought to deal with some of the objections to its deceased antecedent. It gave more power to the Assembly than had at first been granted, but of course it still rested on the rock of the sovereignty of the UK Parliament, which from Labour's point of view was the keystone of the fight against the SNP – 'the separatists'. Some of the overriding legislative powers were removed from the Scottish Secretary (who would still be sitting in the Cabinet in London) and the Assembly was to be allowed to have some more control over the way it organised itself. There now began one of the great parliamentary battles of the modern era. Being a constitutional Bill its committee stage was taken on the floor of the Commons, and it lasted for 47 full parliamentary days. Night after night, often into the early hours, the Labour rebels and the Conservative front bench performed the kind of awkward dance you get when cross-party splits are calling the tune. The Nationalists were able to stand back for much of the time, arguing that they had no time for a puny Assembly that wasn't a Parliament. And on the front bench Smith popped up and down like a jack-in-the-box lawyer in a big trial, hour after hour and day after day defending the rather imperfect scheme against all that could be thrown at it. Power devolved is power retained, said Enoch Powell time and again. You couldn't have two Parliaments in a sovereign state: it was Union or Independence. Tam Dalyell asked what came to be the West Lothian Question – after devolution, how was it that he would be able to vote at Westminster on, for example, education as it affected the voters of a constituency in Surrey but not as it affected his own constituents, education being a matter devolved to the Assembly? The answer, Smith sometimes said in irreverent private moments, was simply 'So what?'

They were an extraordinary stage army, the denizens of the devolution debate. At the heart of it were the serious arguments between Francis Pym and Leon Brittan for the Tories and Smith for the Government, but from every side there were strange distractions. Should Shetland be exempted, because it preferred London Government to the likely Edinburgh variety? What precisely would be the role of the judicial committee of the Privy Council in this new set-up, an argument which gave that august constitutional body a moment in the sun? How many Scottish MPs would be allowed to come to Westminster? And would there be proportional representation for the Assembly, the demand of the Liberals who had now secured a tenuous foothold on power through the Lib-Lab pact of 1977?

It all foundered on the referendum and the coming together of rebel forces on the question of whether a simple majority should be enough to enact constitutional change. A threshold was introduced which would in effect render a narrow Yes majority invalid and would oblige the Government to introduce a repeal order in the Commons. On the night

35

the 40 per cent amendment was passed – requiring the Act to have the consent of four out of ten of all those entitled to vote – there were scenes of near farce in the Commons. The Deputy Speaker, appropriately enough a former Lord Provost of Glasgow, Sir Myer Galpern, had at one stage to send the Serjeant-at-Arms into the voting lobby with his sword to flush out offending members who had been accused of holding up a vote as part of a complicated piece of skulduggery to help the Government.

The Government Whips, though several of them regarded devolution privately as if it were some unknown virus that had arrived from a distant planet, used every trick they knew to get the Bill through. Smith stayed on the side of propriety, just, and kept his hands clean. There were some things the deputy chief whip, Walter Harrison, thought it better for him not to know. But he knew or suspected most of them anyway.

By the end of the parliamentary passage of the Bill and in the referendum campaigns that followed, Smith and his party had learned a lot. It became clear that the Government was falling apart, wallowing in serious economic difficulty and facing the Winter of Discontent with the unions. As if economic troubles were not enough, a huge constitutional issue had opened up deep divisions in the party which seemed unlikely to heal quickly. Outside Scotland, the devolution debate had gone on fairly quietly. It was hardly the stuff of discussion among Surrey commuters. But Labour had almost cracked on the issue, and Welsh MPs were furious because they knew perfectly well what was about to happen in the referendum – that it would be thrown out by a vast majority – and that their Government would be humiliated. All this with Mrs Thatcher in full cry, awaiting her moment.

And in Scotland the weaknesses of the Government's devolution case were about to be revealed. In the referendum, Labour and the SNP were supposed to be on the same side, campaigning for a Yes. But of course their activists had had their daggers drawn for years, and in many seats barely spoke to each other during the campaign, let alone co-operated. The problem was obvious: Labour said vote Yes because it was the only way to stop a drift to independence, and the SNP said vote Yes because it was the best way to get independence. Once a Parliament was set up it would demand more powers said the SNP and Labour. Anti-devolutionists argued the same case using Tam Dalyell's famous 'slippery slope' as the picture of the path to eventual independence that would open up. It was a deeply uncomfortable campaign for Labour, and no-one who saw him will forget Smith handing out leaflets in the last days to a half-hearted electorate which was more interested in the economy and unemployment and thought little of a Government which by that time had lost much of its will to live.

It was Yes, by a whisker. But on the issue of the repeal which now had to be introduced because the 40 per cent threshold hadn't been reached, Callaghan hesitated and the SNP decided to force a vote of confidence. The group was split but the majority ignored the warnings of the disaster that might lie ahead and put down the motion. Mrs Thatcher followed up in an instant and on a famous March night the Government lost by one vote and entered an election campaign which in its heart it knew it would lose.

Smith by this time had had a few months in the Cabinet as Trade Secretary, his devolution work done, but as he saw the Government go down he was back in those long nights of the Scotland Bill committee stage, or watching the months of proceedings in the Lords, hearing Tam Dalyell's sighs from the bench just behind him, listening to another Kinnock speech from the backbenches putting an eloquent case against it all. It had been a bruising passage for him, but in the end a political victory. Defeat in the referendum was bitter – the atmosphere in Edinburgh on that March Friday was black when the results came in and people knew that it was not enough. But there was a certain exhilaration to be found soon afterwards in Smith. He was free of a political task which had probably been impossible from the start, but it had established him in the first rank of his party. Ministers who had worked with him knew he had parliamentary skills, and sensitive political antennae, and even those who had excoriated him from the backbenches for perpetrating a piece of bad Government knew that he was only doing a job.

Yet the experience had been more for the party and for him than a failed parliamentary effort. The rather reluctant reformer of his early years, when he sat beside Willie Ross, had changed. He was now more willing to convert his instincts as a Scot into a political form. In the years that followed there would be no backsliding – and indeed he would come to concede quite quickly what had never been allowed for in the Scotland Bill, tax-raising powers for the Assembly. These were the years when Smith's political attitudes settled into the pattern that would mould a Shadow Chancellor and Leader.

He had political ruthlessness, the natural civilised brutality of the lawyer, strengthened now by the experiences of the Scotland Bill. There was a greater commitment than before to a reforming programme for Government. But, as the post-election arguments began and the succession to Callaghan became the issue in the party, there was also a strengthening of the views he had held for 20 years.

Scottish politics at Westminster had strained the party but it was economic policy which became the principal issue on which Right and Left began their titanic struggle after 1979, and it would be some time before a backward glance would confirm how what had happened on devolution between 1976 and 1979, in a Government which is largely remembered for mistakes and for being the last gasp of an old order, would play some part in the changing attitudes and modernising of Labour that was to come.

By the start of the Eighties, Smith was like so many in his party – he knew that what lay ahead would be grim, and that party argument would be bloodstained for years. But he knew something else, that even if those who held more traditional views prevailed, nothing could ever be the same again.

THE NIGHTMARE

Labour sleepwalked into the Eighties. The party was hardly conscious, because the battering from Mrs Thatcher was proving so fierce and because on top of it there was the sound of war in constituencies up and down the country where the drums were beating an insistent tune. Those who argued that they had been betrayed were not only going to take revenge, but saw the chance to shape the party anew.

In the next two years there was to be a leadership election, a divisive and poisonous deputy leadership election, the defection of three leading Cabinet ministers from the last Government and the foundation of the SDP. Tony Benn was rampant, at the height of his powers as the best orator in modern politics – convincing constituency parties that the right response to the failures of 1974–79 and defeat by Mrs Thatcher was fundamentalism. For Smith and those like him they were years of retreat.

Indeed, he retreated in quite a practical manner. Although he was in the Shadow Cabinet and he played a nominal role in some of the groups set up on the old Right to fight the Bennite Left he didn't try to become a public bruiser in the way that Denis Healey did, before and after his narrow squeak when Benn nearly removed him from the deputy leadership in 1981. Smith spent more time at the Bar during parliamentary recesses – he would joke about scouring the papers at Easter for a good murder that might come to court in the summer – and he took the chance to spend a little more time with his young family in Edinburgh.

He certainly fought for Healey. He had supported him against Foot for the leadership in 1980, a tilt which Foot never for a moment regarded as disloyalty by his old ministerial junior because he knew like everyone else that Smith's position was roughly the same as it had been a decade earlier. He had never shown any inclination to move leftwards, though there would be some good arguments in the Shadow Cabinet in later years about precisely what constituted a left-wing or radical stance in the party of the late Eighties.

If anyone in Smith's position had sought a moment in which his political position would be solidified and clarified, here it was. The hard Left was sweeping through many constituencies and winning votes at party conference which made fundamental changes in the party's rules and its programme. Smith was against them all. He had fought unilateralists in Glasgow in the Fifties; he had been a Gaitskellite. So there was no reason to shrink from the battle against Benn – although in one of the curiosities that make politics still a human business, the two men always preserved a friendly relationship. They had been happy ministers together at the Department of Energy and although they had almost nothing political in common by the early Eighties they retained an affection, a fact which was obvious in Benn's tribute after Smith's death. But for Smith, as for Healey and Hattersley and the rest, the Bennites were the enemy. And then there was the problem of the SDP.

In this episode, so traumatic in Labour's life, the character of Smith's politics emerges. He had generally gone along with Shirley Williams and Bill Rodgers in Government – for the last few months, in Cabinet – but had frankly never much liked David Owen. They found themselves on the same side often enough, but when the Gang of Three started to stir up the party in 1980 Smith was furious. It was a collision of old loyalties, and he made an instinctive choice. He backed the party. No-one who knew him could have expected anything else.

Since he had joined he'd been on the Right. His support for Gaitskell was straightforward. His happy alliances with the old machine in Glasgow to fight the troublesome Left seemed quite natural to him. But it was not a pragmatism without ideals, not simple rough ambition with nothing more. After all, he had been faced soon after he came into Parliament with the crisis on Europe and it would have been easier to read the three-line whip and march into the Aye lobby than join Roy Jenkins – who resigned as deputy leader on the issue – and with 68 other Labour MPs give Heath his Bill and take Britain into Europe. He did not do it out of any particular loyalty to Jenkins, and never became part of his circle afterwards. Indeed he developed then an attitude which he retained for the rest of his life, a slight disdain for the Jenkinsites who went on to found the SDP with the support of those clustered around David Owen (who were a quite different breed).

When the struggle led the Gang of Three to leave Labour in early 1981, with Jenkins now back from the Commission Presidency in Brussels, it put many Labour right-wingers in an awkward position. Some struggled with their consciences, and if Benn had beaten Healey and become deputy leader in 1981, many more would certainly have defected to the new party. But Smith was offended when anyone suggested that he might have considered such a thing. It seemed clear at the time that he would rather have left Parliament than join another party.

He used to say in those days that he had been trying to work out what it was that made him feel uncomfortable with the SDP and comfortable with Labour, for all its troubles. He'd concluded that it was that he felt at home with trade unionists and they did not. That was rather a crude divide but a telling one. In Smith there was a genuine classlessness which he could hardly define but was there. Alongside it was a loyalty to old Labour ways, the links with the unions which had been so useful in the battles of the Sixties, later in the battles against the SNP, and would be just as helpful, he hoped, in the struggle with Benn. So it was part Labour loyalty, part social outlook that made him deeply unsympathetic to the new party. He thought his instinctive attitude was confirmed by the calibre of some (though not all) of the breakaway MPs, which was very poor.

For Labour's very survival it was important that people like Smith never blinked when the convulsion came. Healey, Hattersley, Smith and the others of that ilk thought Williams by far the most serious loss and they knew that they would be lucky to escape without an even more damaging haemorrhage. They regarded Foot's amiable but erratic leadership as more or less a complete disaster, and were preparing already for what might follow.

As long as the Labour Party exists there will be arguments about what would have happened if Healey had become leader instead of Foot. It's argued in some quarters – Hattersley has said it for years – that the SDP episode would have been avoided, Bennery could have been defeated and Labour would have returned to a more normal life, after a few adventures. To those of us who watched it from outside at the time that argument seems difficult to sustain. Before the leadership election the frustration and anger on the Left had become intense. Healey the bruiser would have tackled it resolutely, but he would have faced formidable forces. Benn would have been no less eloquent in those circumstances, and would probably have found it much easier to make ground against the ex-Chancellor who had many old enemies from pay policy days in powerful positions in the unions. The National Executive Committee would have voted consistently against the leader; he would have lost important conference votes. Appeals to the party at large over the heads of the activists would have inflamed things even more. As a recipe for an SDP – perhaps a stronger one than existed – it would have been perfect. The defections would have been delayed, but there might have been many more when they came.

The two years from the foundation of the SDP to the lost general election of 1983 were for Labour a nightmare almost without a chink of daylight to lighten the gloom. A hard Budget in 1981 and rising unemployment made Mrs Thatcher unpopular, but not as unpopular as Foot. And then came the Falklands war, a *deus ex machina* whose arrival could not have been better timed from the Government's point of view since it eclipsed Jenkins less than a month after he was elected as MP for Hillhead in Glasgow and put Foot, the disarmer, in a position where he couldn't win the public argument and was forced to offend many in his party by taking what he believed was a proper position of patriotism. If it had been true in 1979 that things could never be the same for Labour again, how much more it was true now.

After election defeat and Foot's inevitable resignation Smith was back in a familiar position, organising a campaign, this time for

Hattersley. But it soon become clear that he would lose heavily to Kinnock whose freshness was exhilarating to the party. His victory, crowned by his cry of 'Never again' as he spoke about the election defeat to the party conference, meant that a new course had been set. Kinnock had broken with the hard Left in 1981 over Benn's deputy leadership campaign and he was privately angry with himself for having put Foot through the agony of his failed leadership by campaigning for him. He really meant never again.

At this point Smith's story and the story of the modern Labour Party can be seen to start to wind together. Kinnock knew from his painful experiences watching Foot's leadership disintegrate that he had to be tough, and he knew that it depended on having some supporters in the Shadow Cabinet who were not from the Left. Smith was there. The problem was that someone like him, respected by his colleagues and well known to the unions, hardly registered as a champion of the constituencies. In his one effort to reach the NEC, in 1983, when he stood in the constituency section which was dominated by the hard Left, he got the support of only a couple of dozen constituency parties. It was clear that election defeat hadn't turned the tide in that quarter.

All the more reason for the Hattersley team to rally to Kinnock. Smith did so quite happily, though he and Kinnock were hardly similar. They dressed in a different way, their social styles were different, they spoke a different kind of political language. And yet they came together for the many bumps and scrapes in the period after 1984 when it began to dawn on the party that Kinnock was more serious about reform than they had imagined. He used to say to his colleagues that they'd seen nothing yet, and that he would continue to surprise them. On party affairs, he did.

It was a period in which the Shadow Cabinet could start to feel that the worst was behind them. Kinnock was ruthlessly moving the centre of power from party headquarters to the Commons (though some of his colleagues thought too much of it was going straight to his office) and policy – on Europe, for example – was being so heavily rewritten that the 1983 manifesto began to feel like a part of ancient history. Smith had his reservations about aspects of Kinnock's leadership but he could feel happier than he had for years, though the centre of gravity on the front bench was now firmly among the Kinnockite Left, with whom he could never feel as entirely comfortable as he had on a front bench dominated by what had once been called the Right. He was trusted by the leader to be in the frontline, and as Shadow Trade and Industry Secretary he had the good fortune to find the issue which would mark him out as one of the opposition's smartest performers – Westland.

The crisis was brief but it shook the Government. The almost-forgotten details of the struggle between Leon Brittan and Michael Heseltine caused Thatcher more political trouble in her second term than any other single event. Heseltine walked out of the Cabinet in a famous huff, and Brittan was forced to resign in humiliating circumstances over his connivance with Number 10 in the leak of a law officer's letter to discredit Heseltine. Throughout the affair Smith was at his best, interrogating in his courtroom manner and breaking off at will to share jokes with his own backbenches. He had been performing well through the last year. This seemed to mark him as Labour's star Commons performer.

And to cap it, Kinnock chose this moment to make a bad speech. He has since admitted that he knew it was a dud almost from the moment he started, and this was on the day on which Mrs Thatcher was facing a potential rebellion and a speech from Heseltine on the backbenches that could have greatly weakened her grip on power. Kinnock flopped, Heseltine made as polite a speech as was possible in the circumstances (except with reference to Kinnock) and the moment had passed.

But it had its effect on Labour. Smith, the man who had run Hattersley's campaign against Kinnock, was now the Leader's best parliamentary performer. Though he struggled to bring any first to set-piece platform speeches – his conference performances in those years seldom stirred anyone up – in the Commons he was a devastating turn. He could make Labour MPs feel optimistic that they could still win some battles even if they thought it likely that they were about to lose their third general election in a row. As indeed they were.

These years in Opposition had gained them nothing at the polls. After eight years of misery, Thatcherism was in command and the danger for Labour was that there were ominously consistent signs that many of their voters felt they had grown out of an old-fashioned party and had no intention of coming back. Kinnock's reforms had not yet convinced them, and the fresh new look – this was the election of the red rose and the Kinnock film – had not eclipsed their worries about Labour's tax plans, about which Hattersley, as Shadow Chancellor, and his Leader appeared muddled and unconvincing.

It was in that atmosphere that Smith began to be spoken of as a Shadow Chancellor. He was known as a reliable Commons performer, and his caution was thought to be a natural balance to Kinnock's effervescence. His rise became inevitable.

Shadow Chancellors can win and lose elections. When Smith was appointed in 1987 it was to produce an economic policy – and perhaps even more importantly a policy on personal taxation – that could stop Labour losing on the issue which, above all others, had cost it votes in 1987. In one sense his very appointment was a reassurance to the public. He wore sensible suits and spoke like a man who never opened his mouth without thinking first. He was the natural choice for what was, the Leader's aside, the most difficult job in his party.

THE TAX MAN

Labour knew that if an election against Mrs Thatcher was going to be won the middle classes had to start believing that they could vote Labour without starting to become poorer the day after the election. Every poll told the same story. The electorate feared the consequences of Labour's spending plans on their taxes, and it was a fear that had proved impossible to erase in the 1987 campaign. The story of Smith's Shadow Chancellorship is really the story of the Shadow Budget before the 1992 election.

The sensitivity about the tax issue can hardly be exaggerated. In 1987 the old bogey had returned, with Kinnock and Hattersley apparently saying different things – or at least not being sure at any moment what the other was saying. Each admitted afterwards that a better script had to be ready for next time. When Smith took over he knew that he would be judged on presenting a 'responsible' Labour programme at the next election and, he must have known, any leadership prospects depended on getting it right.

Much would come before, but it was the event that was Smith's own and a kind of summation of his politics. It was controversial in the party, some believing that it contributed to the fourth election defeat in a row, and it has become an episode which Labour will still be pondering when the strategy for the next election is drawn up. In it were the characteristics of Smith – clarity, comprehensibility and straightforwardness. On those counts it can hardly be faulted, especially compared with what had gone before. The issue is whether there was any alternative to the clear identification of the extent of the coming tax rises for the better off, and how far that contributed to John Major's victory. In the phrase that Margaret Thatcher used to characterise the Eighties – was there any alternative?

It was Smith's own plan. There was never any doubt from the start about his authority, not least because Kinnock's leadership had a couple of troubled years before and after the 1987 election. Although no-one seriously proposed a coup there was plenty muttering. Smith was naturally a beneficiary of this, because he was beginning to appear the likely safest successor. Attention of that sort was flattering (no politician of any standing will object to being thought of as a natural leader) but it was awkward. The relationship with Kinnock was usually placid, and often quite warm, but it had a number of spectacular rocky moments.

These were years when everybody became a reformer. Smith was now ready to go along. Although he had a traditionalist's affection for union machines – they had been so useful in the past, and how would the Scottish Labour Party work without them? – he had learned in the collapse of the Callaghan Government and the party struggles afterwards that there was no alternative to the kind of programme Kinnock was proposing. The Leader had already set his hand to organisational reform, and that would go much further, but he had also decided on the policy reviews which would take everyone into uncharted waters.

It was the collision of the urge to reform and the urge to be clear on tax that placed a little landmine under the election campaign. After '87 the policy reviews were to give Labour a new look. Red roses were fine – though some members of the Shadow Cabinet always looked uncomfortable with them, and found it hard to wave a stem with enthusiasm, even in front of a big crowd. But policy had to be overhauled. And it was in 1989 that the search for a fundamental policy framework led to part of the Shadow Budget being written with hardly anyone aware of it.

There it is in the campaign document *Meet the Challenge, Make the Change*, a glossy publication which was supposed to represent the triumph of Kinnockism. Clear, sensible policies stripped of ambiguity and the evidence of a modern party. It included a pledge on pensions and on benefits which was to cost a Labour Government something over £4 billion. It had been agreed in Smith's policy review group that the pensioners' increase should not be less than had been agreed in 1987. But by the time *Meet the Challenge, Make the Change* was published and the spending commitments were baldly stated, it was clear that the airy assumptions about Government surpluses had been made too easily and they were stuck with pledges which would greatly affect the policy on tax.

The option of retreat from the pledges was discussed. Not only would it be embarrassing, and a gift to the Government, but this was the time of the Lawson boom. To be seen to be pulling back from such commitment at a time of prosperity – though it would not be long before recession – was politically impossible. Smith was stuck with it.

There were moments when he could have stopped it and did not. But for an important period of the discussions on the policy reviews he was away from Westminster after the heart attack which he suffered just after the party conference in October 1988. For several months he was concerned more with a proper recovery and exercise – the famous hillwalks increased in number – than what at the time seemed policy minutiae. They may have been a cloud no bigger than a man's hand then; but they would overshadow the election itself.

The moment when something could have been done was when recession came. It would have been possible to prepare the ground for scaling down commitments. It wasn't done. In retrospect that decision, or omission, was expensive. Anything which could have opened up the tax and spending plans at election time would have been helpful to Smith, since he was already committed to an economic regeneration programme and as things stood it was going to be considerably smaller than the instant, promised increases in pensions and benefits. Politically, the balance seemed wrong for three years before the election.

Although the Treasury team was by this time quite sizeable, and there was a group of reputable economists and ex-Treasury civil servants and advisers, it was a nervy business. The Conservatives decided in their earliest planning for the election that tax would be their issue, partly because they remembered their history and knew of Labour's difficulty in explaining precisely who would pay more tax and how much. It had always been the confusion as much as the thought of increases that had alarmed voters. So their research told them, and Labour believed it too.

So in the summer of 1991 David Mellor, who was then the Treasury Chief Secretary, began the attack on Labour's spending plans, which he calculated at more than £35 billion. This was good news for Smith. He could say that the figures were clearly an exaggeration and there was enough independent comment supporting him. What he feared was that a properly costed independent study, if the Conservatives had decided to commission one, might have come up with a more realistic figure – somewhere between £20 and £25 billion – which would have been harder to dismiss and would have led to awkward questions on tax. But it was bad enough. By Christmas there had been a VAT scare, and the Conservatives had successfully laid the ground for their Spring campaign. Ministers were still deeply unpopular and many of them were privately despairing of their election chances but they were understandably falling back on the tactics that had worked before.

They were assisted by a characteristic Labour blunder. After five years in which the point of economic policy had been to produce a script from which everyone could read without making mistakes, the election year of 1992 began with a muddle. The Government seized on the episode as evidence of Labour's nervousness about tax, and of course they were right. It was precisely because everyone was so anxious to get it right that the accident happened.

It came about despite long preparations to avoid such a problem. Smith's purpose in the discussion of the previous three years or so had been to agree principles that wouldn't change. There would clearly have to be tax rises for some. That would be defended as proper redistribution. But they would be pitched at a level which would seem fair to most voters, or so Labour hoped. Smith had no doubts about it. Redistribution seemed to him one of Labour's tasks – his traditionalism embraced the sense of 'a fairer society', and that meant fairer taxes.

But the question that had been asked, almost despairingly, in the opposition parties after 1987 was whether it was possible to propose any increase in taxes and be elected. So effective had Thatcher governments been at raising the expectations of tax cuts, and prosperity on the back of them, that even when Labour argued that for the average family the tax burden (taking indirect taxes into account) had risen since 1979, it seemed to make no difference. So when attention focused on the abolition of the ceiling on National Insurance contributions, and the cost on higher wage earners – this was, in the Conservatives' phrase, the hidden tax – there was some pressure to pull back.

In January 1992, with the Tory poster campaign already getting rough, Kinnock's advisers began to be attracted by the idea of phasing the NI changes to mitigate the effect of the changes on higher earners. Kinnock and Smith discussed it and Kinnock wrote to him floating the idea, among others. But before a scheduled meeting to talk it over again, Kinnock went to a prearranged dinner at an Italian restaurant with a group of journalists. The meal was supposed to be a gentle affair. Glenys Kinnock was there. It was mainly about keeping relations going with some journalists thought to be reasonably fair-minded. But it came closer than anything else in his five years as Shadow Chancellor to forcing Smith's resignation. He would probably not have gone, but his rage was such that it probably crossed his mind in the aftermath of what became known as the Luigi's affair, an event that sends a shudder through those who were involved.

As far as can be ascertained Kinnock mused at the table, but in very broad terms, about the possibility of phasing. He certainly did not state it as a new policy. But it came up in conversation. The version of the story that most now believe is that in a taxi going back to the Commons his press secretary, Julie Hall, elaborated to some of those who had been at the dinner, and gave the impression that there was indeed a change of policy.

As the story filtered out, Smith went off like a Roman candle. He couldn't do his job under these circumstances; it was undermining the whole exercise which had taken years to put together; everything had been calculated and approved by the economic advisers; phasing in any case was something which wouldn't make much difference to taxpayers. And so on. He stomped off to Kinnock's room for what could have been a climactic encounter, though it is hard to imagine Smith resigning with an election only a few months away. It would have been a blow to his party which would have left him with the label of betrayer for the rest of his career.

But he was angry. Kinnock, however, was in a mood to apologise. He believes that the story as it came to be written up by the weekend, a few days later, misrepresented what he had said but when Smith arrived he did what had to be done in the circumstances. He apologised. By the time Smith came back to his office he had calmed down.

The incident encapsulated all the tensions of the time. Tax was sensitive, and the problem hadn't yet been solved. Labour's commitment to its spending plans meant that the better-off would have to pay more – but how many? The high-spending label was once again fixed to Labour, despite years of work on precise costing and the pruning of commitments (with the important exception of pensions and child benefit). Finally, it touched on the delicate relationship between Kinnock and Smith. Little wonder that it was the talk of politics.

Kinnock had been wounded by defeat in 1987, and was depressed by his see-saw relationship with the press. Any mistake and a shoal of profiles appeared which were highly critical of his leadership. In that atmosphere there was muttering among some Labour MPs about whether it would make more sense to have a new leader before the next election. Some of those around Kinnock saw the hand of Smith in this: there is no solid evidence for it at all. But it was not lost on those around the Shadow Chancellor that he was seen in the party as a natural successor. Gordon Brown had topped the poll for the Shadow Cabinet in 1988 ahead of Smith but it was the older man, despite his association with the Right in pre-modernising days, who was seen by many Labour MPs as having the weight to be Leader.

This ran as a consistent story for years, bubbling away under the surface and popping up whenever there was a difficulty for Labour. It irritated Smith and it caused some of those around Kinnock – though usually not the Leader himself – to believe that it was not being crushed enthusiastically enough by the Shadow Chancellor's office. This is the kind of problem in politics to which there is no solution. Smith and Kinnock simply had to live with it. Statements of loyalty are nearly always counterproductive. And staff, loyal aides and bag carriers who have given themselves to the service of one man, are sensitive to the merest rumour. Politics at that level, even in Opposition, is in part a game of rivalries. There is sometimes no denying it; it has to be accepted, and the grinding of a rumour mill is simply one of the insistent background noises that become part of life.

Labour approached the 1992 election with high hopes. Smith regarded Norman Lamont as a good target – though his pre-election Budget, with the Shadow Budget in pipeline, was a clever move in what had become a poker game between him and Smith. Instead of going for a reduction in the standard rate he helped lower earners with a reduced rate band, and it caused a certain rewriting of Labour's response on the spot. But Lamont was felt not to be popular, a judgement vindicated in time, and the polls gave Labour a consistent lead. So there was a confidence they hadn't known in a pre-election period before, and the Shadow Budget was to be its underpinning.

Smith took his team to the steps of the Treasury, a rather unSmith-like piece of theatre, and held up a box with his calculations in it. And for a few days it worked exactly as had been intended. Labour was praised for being clear and responsible in spending, and fair on tax. Most taxpayers would gain a little, a few would lose a lot. It was after a week or so that the tide turned, and the comment focused on the losers. They were those who had done rather well out of Thatcherism, and it was said that they had no reason to vote Labour because their gains were going to be frittered away. The rather modest package to boost the economy was hardly a talking point. It had been kept low because of the old troublesome pension and benefit pledges and the necessity to 'balance' the Budget for reasons of 'responsibility'. So a theme in the campaign became the losers. And the argument of fairness, delivered in Smith's characteristically straightforward and rather downbeat way, was portrayed in unfriendly quarters as envy dressed up as policy.

Afterwards, in defeat, various candidates were put forward as explanations. One was the Sheffield rally the week before polling which had looked too triumphalist and which had prompted a Kinnock burst of excitement which looked odd on television (despite the Leader's irritation at the way the rally had been staged). Another was the Shadow Budget. It was the old argument. How specific should you be? Smith had tried to correct the failures of 1987 by trying to make sure that every tax pledge had been worked out and no loose spending pledges were thrown around. But of course it meant that the tax consequences for every voter were clear. Will I be paying more under Labour, Mr Smith? Yes. So many of the beneficiaries of Thatcherism, for all their discontents at a time of recession, did not flood back to Labour in sufficient numbers.

It raised a fundamental question of trust. Was it better, having reformed so much in the party, to count on public confidence returning to Labour or instead to accept that a belt-and-braces Budget had to be prepared to give an answer to every question? Smith always believed he had been right, and it was to influence the way he led the party in the two years that followed.

Despite the election defeat it was his belief that credibility had been restored. Labour had been seen to be arguing about spending commitments and priorities, and not spraying promises across the land. Tax plans, with their traditional hiccups and confusions, had been better constructed than before. And the party was more disciplined, not least by a fourth, hard defeat. Was that not a recipe for steadiness? And in turning straight to Smith when Kinnock resigned the day of his defeat was not the party doing so because he promised a steady course? He believed so, and it was why he led the party as he did.

LEADER

Dull campaigns take the sap out of politics, and by the time John Smith was elected Leader in the high summer of 1992 the Labour Party was drained. Before the tremors of election night had been shaken off, union leaders had made his election a near-certainty with their declarations of support and Bryan Gould's campaign was never more than an attempt to keep a debate alive. If calm was what was wanted, it came. As everyone dispersed on holiday and tried to forget it all, the easy victory held the danger that Smith's leadership would begin in a kind of political torpor. And it did.

Despite John Major's victory, the defeated party Smith led was quite different from the one Neil Kinnock had inherited after the 1983 election. He had to embark then on a revolution which he knew would take at least five years to change the way the party ran itself and the way it made policy. Smith was the beneficiary of those changes, giving him a quiescent National Executive, a reformed conference and a party schooled in realism. The issue was whether that could guarantee the period of steadiness that had seemed to be the case for Smith as leader or whether another convulsion had to come. Smith, as cautious by nature as the day he came into politics, chose to play for time and in doing so he set the tone for his leadership.

This was a peak in his career which he believed would lead to the summit himself, and from that first summer his strategy was preparation for Government. Judging his leadership, at the culmination of a long career, is judging whether he found the right balance between the demands he hoped to face in the future and the present exigencies of Opposition, always fuelled by the frustrations of those who couldn't wait to escape its restrictions.

In the course he pursued he was utterly true to himself, making his moves in the way he had taught himself in the years of Government and 13 long years in the Shadow Cabinet. There would be no impetuosity, no loose talk, much discipline and a strategy that was geared to exploit the Government's mistakes. This was the approach of a political manager drawing up a game-plan, and it had nothing of the gambler in it. That side of him he kept for private political bets (on which, especially in younger days, he'd done rather well). But the energy built up in the party in the late Eighties for more modernisation wasn't going to dissipate, and it was finding a way of absorbing it that proved a great difficulty.

The first decision came early. Should he push on with the one-member-one-vote plan for party elections which was the natural conclusion of the Kinnock reforms? In the Shadow Cabinet, Gordon Brown and Tony Blair, the twin engines of modernisation, said Yes. Smith consulted the unions, took soundings, and said No. It would have to wait a year. Now there is no evidence at all that he was cool about the need for reform. He simply believed he would lose, and the consequences were obvious. Defeat would probably be the end of his leadership.

His decision frustrated some colleagues who believed that there was something almost approaching a moral imperative in pressing on quickly: if the leadership were seen to hesitate, wouldn't the opponents of reform in the unions be strengthened? There was more than tactics involved. There was a question of boldness. Others were thirsty for it now.

So the first few months were defensive in that sense. They involved delay. Smith was acting in character. However pressing the enthusiasm of colleagues for a change in policy he would resist if his instincts told him he might fail. Risks were only to be taken when there was no alternative. Instead he started to try to define his leadership in the public mind not so much by a series of decisions – changes in the party or its policies – but by marking out territory which he felt instinctively to be his own.

This was the idea of putting moral values back into politics. In the midst of all the party argument about how fast to modernise and whether – in the jargon of the day – 'one more heave' by the old party would win power, Smith was changing the tone. It reflected two sides of the personality that had been remarkably unchanged in a long political career – the obligations of his Christian faith and his belief that Labour must never discard all its traditional language on matters of social justice. Poverty had to be talked about, and so did the redistribution of wealth.

By the time his leadership came along the old Right-Left labels had started to look ridiculous. Apart from a certain historical value in describing where someone had come from, they couldn't cope with the problems of modernisation. Smith, for example, was conservative about some aspects of the modernisers' plans but rather radical in what he was prepared to say about the obligations of a left-of-centre party. Perhaps more than anyone around him had expected, he began to develop a distinctive moral tone in his speeches.

It became obvious. The impressionist Rory Bremner created a caricature of Smith in a pulpit, all beetling brows and stern gaze, delivering a sermon. It was not unfriendly, considering what some of his other victims had to take, and Smith found it not at all offensive, though slightly puzzling. Like many Scots he found it mystifying that humourlessness should always be part of the caricature especially when, as Donald Dewar reminded everyone at his funeral, he could start a party in an empty room, and frequently did.

That was one side. And Bremner managed to touch on the other. He portrayed Smith on one occasion as a regulator, in the mould of the man from OFWAT or OFGAS, talking to the public on behalf of Her Majesty's Opposition. He spoke, he said, for OFGOV. If there were any complaints he would see that they were brought to the attention of the proper authorities. That is exactly the murmur that was beginning to circulate in the party, that Labour was in danger of seeming too complacent, not fiery enough; to be too established in the style of an Opposition that perhaps expected to stay there.

It irritated Smith, for obvious reasons. He had seen and felt the traumas of Labour in the Eighties and he was determined that the party would be steadied to face the next election without risk of capsizing again. Moreover, he had seen a Government collapse from the inside in 1978–79 and he detected the signs on the front bench opposite him. It was sensible for Labour to wait its moment. Indeed, in his first few outings at the despatch box as Leader in autumn 1992 he mounted some grand economic assaults which reminded his party of what he could do in the Commons.

He never had doubts about the strategy. It was sensible to wait for your moment and not to hurry. Party reform must progress, but not at the risk of humiliating defeat. Labour had to be ready for Government. In that respect he was the ex-minister again, thinking of strategies for power. This was probably one of the reasons that he tended to hold back in interviews – seldom working on a useful slogan for a headline, for example – and to stress his responsible attitude. It also showed in his tactics on the Maastricht Bill which had more to do with conviction than political advantage.

With the Government floundering on Maastricht, and nearly breaking in two in the storm, Labour could probably have succeeded in forcing a referendum. The Conservative rebels would have backed it. The Liberal Democrats were already committed to it. It would have put the Government in an appalling position. But it would have split Labour too (though less spectacularly) and the referendum, Smith believed, would be lost. For him, a European who had first defied his party on the issue more than 20 years before, that was not an option he was prepared to contemplate. He had over a number of years already manoeuvred Labour into a position of support for the ERM. He was not going to throw away the kind of European union he believed in. So with his old friend George Robertson, who led for Labour on the Bill, he declined to force the issue.

Hard on top of that decision came the moment when party reform could not be postponed. One-member-one-vote had to go through. Smith had been influenced by his colleagues who were impatient – and there had been backbench whispering about inactivity, and from some of those close to Kinnock some semi-public exasperation about what they felt was a slow pace. So the decision was made. From the start it was obvious that it would be hard, but this was the year it had to be done. The plan was that the party would, in effect, be relaunched in 1995 with a new kind of conference to add to the policies and policy machinery which were being rigorously overhauled, for example through the work of the social justice commission. That meant a modern party in which the block vote wasn't simply reduced, as it had been, but was removed.

In Smith's mind the policies (and his tone in explaining them) and the party reforms had always been linked. An election victory required them both, and indeed his argument for having waited a year to start the OMOV campaign was that it increased the chances of success by demonstrating all the aspects of his strategy. Others disagreed, and still do. But the campaign was on.

From the start it was obvious that it would have to be won without John Edmonds of the GMB who was utterly opposed. Smith – who was sponsored by the union – had many meetings to try to win a compromise or change his mind, and got none. By the time conference week came, in Brighton, it was by no means clear that he would win. A certain amount of arm-twisting had been done, and there had been a successful speech at the TUC, but some of the supporters of OMOV complained in those last days that not enough work was being done on delegates. Whatever the truth of that assertion, it became clear on the morning of the vote – the debate having started the day before – that Smith might lose.

51

By lunchtime his staff had taken soundings in the hall, and had got reports from old conference hands that there was something in the air that suggested defeat. Already plans had been laid for that contingency. Smith would tell the NEC that night that he wanted another vote the next day which would be a clear vote of confidence in his leadership. If he lost that one he would resign. He did not believe that he would have lost in a second vote, but he knew that the damage to his standing if he scraped through would be so severe that he probably could not win the election, and might face a difficult leadership challenge before then. So there was an air of desperation around him, although he was memorably cool during a lunch given by the *Daily Mirror* with all around him seeming to melt in near-panic. A last card was played. John Prescott. He was asked, and he agreed, to wind up the debate and in a famous speech, its arguments cleverly directed at constituency activists, he seemed to make the difference. Smith won.

It was the most important moment of his leadership. Defeat would have weakened him so much that he would never again have been able to present himself as the man in charge. Victory was a public demonstration that the party was continuing to change, and it also performed the important function of cooling some of the criticisms from those who had talked of inactivity. The change had been made at last.

But it left difficulties. There were some personal problems. Smith's deputy, Margaret Beckett, had made clear in private her opposition to OMOV and in public had sounded lukewarm, even in the week of the party conference itself. She welcomed the vote, but made little secret of her belief that it was a policy on which it would have been better never to have embarked. Smith and his close colleagues were naturally irritated at her attitude and in the last months there was less willingness to confide in the deputy than there had been before.

And although the OMOV victory had dealt with some of the worries of the modernisers, those who wanted to move still faster were anxious to force the pace.

But only a few months were left. All the preparations of his leadership, and he saw it as a series of preparations for Government, were to be left to someone else. John Smith died on the morning of 12 May.

Many people were shaken and moved to quiet contemplation by what happened next. The awful sadness among friends and colleagues was predictable, the national spasm of grief was not. Far beyond the demands of decency at the death of a popular and respected figure there was a sense of public anguish. No doubt some of the tributes contained exaggerations – he'd have dismissed some of them with a sparkling eye and a wide grin – but something occurred in the aftermath of his death that bears examination.

It was clear at once that people had understood the essence of the man. His deliberate effort to find a moral voice that wasn't sanctimonious had begun to get a response. In the appreciations there was an understanding of what he had tried to do which perhaps was beyond what he might have expected. There was a great deal of talk about public service and social values, exactly the territory on which he had wished to be judged. Though he loved a political scrap, and enjoyed the rough manoeuvre when it was needed, he wanted to lead a party which had settled on a set of principles suitable for our times, which could be articulated in an old language, the language of community and personal obligation. After the strange episode of 'back to basics' which caused the Government trouble a few months before, his determination to use a moral dimension (without straying into the area of personal behaviour) sounded a note that people recognised, like a memory from the past.

No one should look back at that brief leadership without considering the significance of the reaction to his death. The only comparable modern case, of course, is Gaitskell's in 1963, an event which set off tremors in the Labour Party which were still reverberating in the Eighties. Smith's departure is different because he leaves no legacy of the factionalism which bedevilled Labour in the Gaitskell era, but the event is surely going to have a power that lasts.

In the leadership campaign that followed his death the civilised nature of the debate wasn't simply a mark of respect, but a demonstration of the changes that had come. And when Blair won he found he could slip happily into the tone that had been Smith's: on the obligations of Labour and the demands of public life and Government. It's an approach that could have been prepared especially for him. The Left-Right arguments have changed their character, and though there will be struggles and explosions ahead – nothing is surer – it is as if a new era has opened. That is Smith's as well as Blair's achievement.

The record of leadership is one that sits happily beside the political career that preceded it. Consistency was Smith's hallmark. The attitudes he struck as Leader of the Opposition were fundamentally the same as those he took into politics. Some things had changed – he was more open to ideas of constitutional reform (his devolution experience having been a turning point in his attitude to how it must be done) and of course his economic thinking had been changed radically as a result of the Eighties experience. But underneath, the approach was the same. In personality he was the same kind of operator, canny and methodical, resolute when his mind was made up, and loyal to those who had been loyal to him. These were the qualities that brought him into Government, into a position of power in Opposition and finally to the leadership itself.

They were the qualities that provided a happy legacy to his successor, but would they have made a Prime Minister?

He was by nature a man of Government. Public life did not seem to him to be an opportunity to make a mark by exhibiting an attractive personality or perhaps by achieving a few isolated successes which might be attached to your name. It was about power. He enjoyed being a minister. Even in the throes of devolution he was exhilarated, though he knew that if he was seen to have mishandled and the Government fell his career would probably peter out quite quickly. Everyone in the Government enjoys that pulse that throbs through Whitehall and the Cabinet room, but some feel it more strongly than others so that it has almost a life-giving power. Smith was one of them.

His leadership should be seen in that context. He was trying to get his party ready for power. In party reform and on economic policy, the two issues which had to be dealt with before an election campaign could safely be fought, he was determined not to slacken his grip. That caused problems with colleagues and on the backbenches, and there would have been more to come.

Smith may have been a party man in the sense that his loyalty was to Labour people and Labour ideals, but he was never a party insider. If that seems curious, consider how he played a relatively quiet role after the defeat of 1979, how he just dipped his toe once into the stormy waters of the NEC before he became Leader, and how in the machinations over OMOV at the end he seemed to his staff to have been surprised at times by the way the unions were playing it.

He was a political operator, certainly, and fond of jousting in complicated manoeuvres against Michael Heseltine or Nigel Lawson across the despatch box, fond also of pulling off a tactical coup as a minister to win an important vote. Leadership elections apart – he loved those – his political crafts tended to be used for clear purposes. The game for its own sake, or the factional politics which was part of Labour's soul, seemed a bit wearying. As evidence you could look to his own constituency where local jealousies and accusations of corruption turned the by-election campaign of his successor and friend, Helen Liddell, into an embarrassingly close-run thing for Labour. He had simply not involved himself in the politics of the local council, spending his days in the constituency doing the rounds of village halls and backstreets for his surgeries with the people to whom he felt so committed.

All this points to a political outlook which was about objectives – social, economic, moral. Yet 'moral' doesn't quite catch it. Smith was no preacher and no moralist. But he was someone who had felt all his days that without a code of values life was meaningless, and that the point of having values was that they were not private but public.

The strength of his leadership was that he had begun to make that attitude tell, as evidenced by the reaction to his death.

No one can say whether he would have won the next election, though he had come to believe he would. But he remembered well leaving home on a summer morning in 1992 and saying that when he came back he would be Chancellor of the Exchequer. Confidence had been running strong. Three days before polling he had agreed a statement in the Treasury about exchange rate policy, to be issued after the polls closed. After experiences like that, and with knowledge of the vagaries of Government still fresh from earlier days, he was not going to succumb to the belief that it was in the bag.

The argument which will go on is whether that proper caution about the election result should have prompted a different style of leadership, one that did not emphasise so much steadiness. It is now academic, perhaps a matter for the future when the consequences are known.

For now, for everyone who knew John Smith and worked with him, thoughts of the future are fused with memories. I remember first coming to know him in devolution days, those tingling times when great political happenings were afoot and the landscape was stirring with possibilities. Nobody, in any party and of any belief, was unaffected by it. Those of us watching from outside, and down from the reporters' gallery in the Commons, caught something of the sense that infected those who were involved. For Smith it was never a remote political operation, an exercise in Government. It was human. He knew about devolution's doubtful parentage in his party, and knew well that Parliament is a place where individuals are like players across a chessboard, exercising their minds on grand strategies but playing tricks as well. In long nights after the debate had subsided there was a minister who somehow managed to combine an understanding of great purpose with the bubbling good nature of the streetwise lawyer who's just spotted the opening in his adversary's case.

That was the authentic Smith, less complicated than he has sometimes been made to seem. His background gave him the character he would use to shape his career, and his early years shaped a set of beliefs that would remain consistent with him through the years. Policies changed, attitudes did not.

As was recognised in all parties, and by us outside who watch politics at work, there is a legacy from that life which can be cherished beyond the ranks of his own party. The Prime Minister said as much when he died. Some day a settled judgement can be reached on the successes and failures of that brief leadership but not before other events have taken their course.

For now, there is a life that can be celebrated. It was generous and steadfast in its beliefs, and for people in every party and none, outside or inside politics, that is a memory to keep.

Tribute

by

James Gordon

At Cluny Church, Edinburgh, on 19 May, James Gordon paid tribute to his late friend.

John Smith's considerable achievements have been recalled in the many and dignified tributes which have dominated the media since last Friday, and there is no need for me to rehearse them here. These achievements certainly filled the nation with a sense of the cruelty and injustice of death, taking someone in his prime who, on all the available evidence, was poised to achieve the highest office in the land, which a majority of his fellow citizens felt he not only deserved but would enhance. You cannot become a Cabinet minister at 40, and be elected leader of a great political party, without unusual courage, judgement and intellect. His political skills, his mastery of his subject, his wit at the despatch box, were all qualities which rightly commanded respect; but what won the hearts of so many in the nation and caused such an unprecedented outpouring of real grief at his passing were his more personal qualities, his transparent decency, straightforwardness, a keen sense of fairness and a willingness to fight for those not able to speak up for themselves; and, less obtrusive but underpinning all of this, a strong religious faith. John did not allow his undoubted abilities, which marked him out from the rest of men, to distance him from them, and his natural qualities shone through, so that he remained someone people could relate to and trust to understand their problems, and his abilities created the confidence in him that he could, and would, do something about them. He was one of us, not one of them. I suppose if you are unpretentious by nature, the name John Smith, without even a middle name, gets you off to a good start.

For the source of these qualities, which are learned almost passively in childhood, one must go back to Ardrishaig in Argyll and his family life. John's father was a schoolmaster, and probably, together with the local minister and doctor, one of the few men in the entire area with a university education. The fact that his father used that to help others, rather than preen himself as being different, must have influenced young John in his own unpretentiousness and contributed to his high regard for education as an avenue for self-improvement. You don't grow up in a schoolmaster's house learning to worship money or even material advancement.

He had a religious upbringing, although it may well have been the music which attracted him, for he had a fine singing voice. The laughter of his friends as the Leader of Her Majesty's Loyal Opposition would regale us, complete with appropriate mimes and gestures, with some of the Sunday School songs of his childhood is a fond memory.

> Seek them out, get them gone,
> All the little rabbits in the field of corn.
> Envy, jealousy, malice and pride,
> They must never in my heart abide.

John's evident enjoyment as he sang should not obscure the more important point that the essential message of the hymn had certainly got through to John as a child and remained with him throughout his life.

His mother treated any of us who stayed there as though it was an honour to have us in their home. When I last saw her on the occasion of John's silver wedding and Jane's 21st, about two years ago, John had already been elected the previous week as the Leader of the Labour Party. Almost with diffidence she confided to me, 'I'm really very proud of what he has achieved.' John too was proud of his parents and of his two sisters, Mary and Annie, and in particular their artistic abilities. Significantly, paintings by both of them hang in his home.

He had a great love of Argyll whose scenic beauty he felt was seriously under-rated. I understand that members of the Cabinet are asked to leave behind a book for the library at Number Ten, and John was proud of his choice of Neil Munro's *Tales of Para Handy* which immortalises the puffers on the west coast of Scotland.

The next big formative influence on his life was Glasgow University of which he had a deep love and a high regard for its academic traditions, stretching back to 1451. Of course his honours degree in History, followed by an LLB were important. But more important, perhaps, for the MP of the future, were the honing of debating skills in the University Union and his introduction to student politics. Those of us who were contemporaries, in retrospect, tend to endow the whole period with an almost Camelot quality; but, certainly, it produced friendships which have lasted ever since. While some of us preferred a style of oratory designed to rouse passions, perhaps more appropriate to party conferences of either party, John, even then, spoke in a style which would ultimately win him distinction at the despatch box. I suspect that he had an innate distrust of over-flowery language which might lead people to expect things which could not be delivered.

Most important of all, however, it was at Glasgow University that John met Elizabeth. This was truly a marriage made in heaven. It was love at first sight, but the formal engagement took a little longer. At their engagement party, John confided to me, 'Why did I wait so long? I might have lost her.' Elizabeth, who luckily was within earshot responded with that characteristic mixture of laughter and tears which we all associate with her. Without Elizabeth, and later the three girls, John could not have achieved what he did. The Smith women are a formidable team, and I once remarked to him, when he was Shadow Chancellor, that it might be useful evidence of his potential ability to control spending departments. With a wry grunt he pointed out that that might not work if people realised just how unsuccessful he had been.

To all who encountered them, let alone were·close friends, his wonderful, and usually self-deprecating, humour must be added to his many qualities. As we have all tried to support each other through the last week, there have been peals of laughter, as well as tears, as we recalled our many happy times with John. Hopefully, in time, the tears at our present loss will pass but the happy memories will remain always.

John's death has dramatically put politics in perspective for us. But the lesson is not that politics are unimportant, or that John somehow was above them. They were vital to John. He would have sacrificed anything, other than his family or fundamental religious beliefs, for the Labour Party. Media descriptions of backbench MPs as lobby fodder enraged him. He had the highest regard for the often unsung efforts of MPs to achieve small but measurable improvements in the lives of their constituents. John certainly entered Parliament, as MP for North Lanark in 1970, quite content to remain a backbench MP. He believed passionately in the concept of public service, and perhaps the best tribute we can pay is to improve the quality of our public life by trying a little harder to fight for what we know to be right, and to do it, whether in our own communities, jobs, or in the nation's Parliament.

Harold Wilson said that a week is a long time in politics: 15 years in Opposition must have seemed like eternity, yet John always felt that his time would come.

Frequently, death is unexpected. It doesn't come neatly at the end of a paragraph, but often cuts short a life in mid-sentence. At least John Smith had completed the work of readying his party and himself for power, so his death, untimely though it was, at least came at the end of a chapter.

He recognised that in democratic politics you can't get things all your own way. Any group of two or more must, and should, require an accommodation of dissenting views, provided that agreement is maintained on essentials. Conviction and sense of purpose, without a willingness to accommodate dissent, ultimately breeds tyranny. Simply balancing views to reach agreement, without a palpable sense of purpose, leaves people leaderless. John's gift was to hold firm on essentials and to know when to dig his heels in, and yet to be able to accommodate other views on less important matters.

In their tributes to John, I think politicians of all parties enhanced the esteem in which Parliament is held by the nation, and many have said, 'Why can't they behave like that all the time?' Perhaps they would be encouraged to do so if we in the media were to concentrate on the more constructive aspects of politics which goes on all the time inside and outside Parliament, and a little less on confrontation simply because that is easier. John set standards for behaviour in public life, and if the example he set in politics encourages others to mould themselves in his image, the current cynicism about public life would quickly be dispelled.

And now John goes from here back to his beloved Argyll and to be buried on the island of Iona, one of the main centres of Christianity since the year 563. Kings of Scotland, Norway and Ireland are reputed to be buried there, but that would not have provided any attraction for John; indeed, his knowledge of history would have given him considerable reservations about quite a few of them. Without overdosing on Burns, he certainly endorsed the view that 'Rank is but the guinea stamp, a man's a man, for all that.'

He would however have been enormously grateful as I know Elizabeth and the family are, to know that the islanders have been willing to accept him on their island in death as they did in life on his many visits there. It is a suitable final resting place for a good and great man.

John Smith's Socialism:
His Writings and Speeches

by

Gordon Brown

'We will do our best to reward your faith in us but please give us the opportunity to serve our country. That is all we ask.'

These – the last public words I heard from John Smith on the night before his death – are also his political testament.

Public service was, for John, the purpose of politics, with justice as its goal. John passionately believed in a more equal society that would remove the worst of poverty, deprivation and injustice and allow everyone the chance to realise their potential to the full. And the means by which this goal would be achieved was an economic one – no less than the economic renewal of Britain.

John was at his best in the cut and thrust of the House of Commons – logical, incisive and quick-witted, turning the interruptions of his opponents to his own advantage, using them as a foil for his distinctive style. He was never a rabble-rouser; rhetorical flourishes always had to have a purpose. John constructed a case, built an argument, sought through fact and logic to persuade. But powerful arguments were always leavened with humour, which he used to lethal effect as a sharp and piercing instrument of attack, causing delight on his own side and squirming embarrassment and discomfort, often tinged with amusement, on the opposite benches. And this practical and lucid – some said matter of fact – presentation captivated the House of Commons and made the most effective parliamentarian of his generation.

Even in his early student days, in 1960 in an article in his student magazine, he defended debating only in so far as it had a solid purpose. 'It is rather pointless,' he wrote, 'to train people to speak when they have nothing to say.' In his speeches the means – logic, clarity, humour and the quick-fire response – all served the end, that of communicating the message. And communicate he did. Inside and outside the Commons, speaking from the platform of countless conferences and meetings, he was always at his most forceful when he spoke about the issues he cared most about – fairness, justice, opportunity and democratic renewal.

This was as true of his period as Chairman of Glasgow University Labour Club and then in his first by-election candidature, as it was when he was Leader of the Labour Party. In his campaign in the East Fife by-election of 1961, while still only 23, John argued, 'Britain could become a more just community if we had a fairer distribution of wealth,' and went on in his argument that 'people are more important than private profits' to say 'too many expense-account businessmen are able to dodge, leaving the weight of taxation on people of fixed incomes'.

John spoke a great deal about industry policy, about manufacturing, about skills, education and training – 'making Britain's the best educated and best trained workforce in the world'. But behind his call for wealth creation was his ultimate aim of social justice. The purpose of economic revival was to create the wealth to eliminate poverty.

In practical political terms this translated into John's enduring concern with economic prosperity and social justice. He believed they are linked and that one cannot be sustained without the other. That is why he found the 1988 Budget the apotheosis not just of Tory greed but of Tory folly – a wasteful and inefficient use of national resources.

In a speech in 1987, the J.P. Mackintosh memorial lecture entitled 'Prosperity and Justice – the challenge of modern Socialism', he set out his views:

> I wish to argue the case that prosperity, broadly defined as a steadily increasing standard of living in an efficient and productive economy, is not only consistent with a socially just and caring society, but that in an intelligently organised community, prosperity and social justice mutually reinforce each other.
>
> For almost three decades after the Second World War – in what historians may describe as the Era of Full Employment – most Western democracies regarded the maintenance of full employment as not only the obligatory duty of civilised government, but as an indispensable part of a successful economic arrangement. The purchasing power of the employed, for example, was one of the essential mainsprings of demand in the economy. What was socially necessary was rightly also regarded as economically sound. In those times, if it had been predicted that in the late 1980s Britain would have well over three million unemployed and that the then right-wing Government would advertise its economy as successful, disbelief would have been profound.[1]

It was when John talked of social justice, fairness, greater equality, that his words burned with passion. One route to social justice was maximising educational opportunity, and for John it was the most important.

I was given the benefit of a very smart education by the community, which I wouldn't have got if we didn't have a public education system. And if you come from a very ordinary background and get a splendid education then you have an obligation to repay some of that. That's one of the things I feel most strongly about, that people should be given the right to develop their talents as far as they can and as far as they want to, and we should have an opportunist society. And I worry at the moment that education and training is not offered on the scale it should be.

JOHN SMITH'S SOCIALISM: EARLY INFLUENCES

My father was the dominie – the village schoolmaster – in the remote village of Portnahaven on the West Coast of the island [*of Islay*] and my parents lived there in the school house – as I did for the first two years of my life.

But in 1938 my parents apparently thought it prudent to move to the mainland for my arrival into the world and I was born instead in my grandmother's home in the village of Dalmally in Argyll so I regard myself as almost a Hebridean.

John did not write a great deal. Whether as lawyer, debater or politician, he preferred the spoken word, but the early influences on his life can be pieced together from the few articles – like the one quoted above – that he wrote, speeches he made, reminiscences that friends have put down on paper, and stories told by people who grew up with him. And there were three great influences on his life – his faith in the mutual support that even the smallest communities could offer; his belief in education as the escalator of opportunity; and his inherent sense of everyone's equality.

Islay, where John was brought up for the first two years of his life, was central, as John wrote, to his 'philosophy of existence'. He saw all its inhabitants as 'part of its community, bound into its very nature by its isolation'.

John travelled widely and later lived in Glasgow and Edinburgh and worked in London. But such was his affection and respect for the community of his youth that he was never over-impressed by new surroundings, nor was he ever dismissive of the community where he had been brought up.

John described Islay as a 'busy island' and to outsiders that might have appeared surprising. It may have seemed so to John because there were other, even smaller communities in islands nearby. Yet the 'busy island of Islay', large in comparison with its neighbours yet small enough to be familiar in all its details, was a genuine community where it was possible to know everyone. And when John later wrote of Islay as an island of 'bustle and order and organisation' it was because he saw it that way: a neat microcosm of society as a whole. The sense John had of communities supporting their fellow citizens at times of stress or difficulty began with his experience of the Highlands and Islands and never left him. It perhaps explains why he was the first politician to express his outrage at the now notorious statement of Mrs Thatcher that 'there is no such thing as society' when he argued that community and collective action was central to socialism.

Islands captivated John from the beginning to the end of his life – and most of all Iona, the island to which he travelled for family holidays and on which he is now buried. Iona he called 'my favourite island, the location of many happy family holidays'. But Iona was not just an island: it too was a community, and one with some special features. The Iona Community, a religious initiative dating from the inter-war depression, brought unemployed people from Glasgow to restore the ancient cathedral. It still looms large in the life of the island today.

John's father – the second son in a family of five born to a labourer – was the only child in his family given the opportunity of a University education. First Archie went to school on the mainland in Dunoon, then to Glasgow University to read English and Hitory, and in turn became a member of the Glasgow Student Labour Club. It was a course his son John was to follow more than 30 years later.

John's father was to become headmaster of the primary school in Portnahaven on Islay before moving, when John was two, to Ardrishaig near Tarbert. As Neil MacCormick – a student contemporary and lifetime friend – recalled:

> The values of Ardrishaig schoolhouse and the Tarbert village were etched deep into him. He had a deep admiration for his father Archie Smith and his mother Sarah Cameron Smith. The values they stood for were his too, but thought out for himself, not just swallowed whole. His view of the world and his way of being just the same John with all kinds and classes of people were laid down early and never changed in essentials, though he learned much on his way through his studies, his legal practice, his time in Parliament. He combined in a curious way a genuine egalitarianism with a clear sense of his own vocation to the exercise of high office. He combined an awareness of himself as someone special with a competing sense of the specialness of every human being as a unique repository of worth and dignity. Being the son of the schoolhouse seems to have had on him an effect often noted among sons of the manse.

John reflected on his own schooldays with unabashed enthusiasm and the experience shaped his whole political outlook. He was expected to do well. As he later recalled of his father's proddings: 'It was always "Why weren't you top of the class?". In the end it was easier just to be top of the class.' But his own experience of education convinced him of the benefits of expanding educational opportunities for everyone.

John Smith, 1990 (© Dr Nicholas Posner)

Archibald, Sarah and John Smith

Archibald, Sarah and John, Anne and Mary Smith on holiday in Dublin

*John, Mary, Annie, Alastair and their motor car at Dalbuiaich
(August 1953)*

John Smith in 1953

Speaking in Glasgow University Union

GLASGOW TEAM WIN "THE SCOTSMAN" TROPHY

Mr John Smith, of Glasgow University, receives "The Scotsman" Trophy from Mr G. Fraser Cowley, an Assistant Editor of the paper, at the end of the inter-university debating contest in the Marischal College, Aberdeen, last night. With Mr Smith is his colleague, Mr Donald Dewar.

The Glasgow Team win The Scotsman *debating trophy (11 February 1961)*

John Smith, advocate

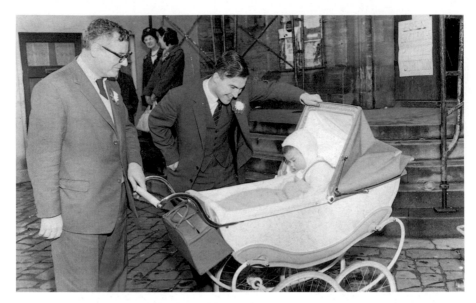

The East Fife by-election, 1961

*Elizabeth Bennett and John Smith celebrate the election of
Chief Albert Luthuli as rector of Glasgow University, 1962*

Elizabeth and John Smith (5 July 1967)

John Smith with Dick Stewart (election agent), John Aitchison, Elizabeth Smith and Margaret Herbeson, June 1970 (©The Scotsman)

Sarah, Elizabeth, Cath, Jane and John outside their family home in Morningside, 1974

John was a member of what he called the 'Highland contingent': the young pupils who moved from small remote Highland schools to Dunoon at the age of 14 for the later years of their secondary education, staying away from home in digs, an experience that was 'OK' as he later recalled, 'for those who are independent and sturdy'. As John wrote:

> There was the Highland contingent which came in for years four, five and six. Now I am proud to say I was one of them. I lived with Mrs McGilip in Alexander Street, Dunoon, up at the back of Dunoon. I think she had been taking in boys from the Highlands for many years. She was a lovely lady who looked after us and was in a sense a mother who looked after all the boys and girls. People who took in children were passed on from one generation to another.
>
> There was that great contingent from Islay who used to arrive. They brought a new influence into the school and they enjoyed the curiosity of being away from home and mixing together in what we thought was the great metropolis of Dunoon, when you thought that McColl's Hotel was the equivalent of the Savoy or the Ritz. Having been frequently since to the Savoy and Ritz, it's not quite.
>
> I went to digs. It sounds a bit rough at the age of 14 but it worked for me . . . we only went home at Christmas and Easter. You went by boat. There was actually a boat came from Ardrishaig to Gourock in those days, otherwise you went through a complicated system of buses or got picked up by car. But we didn't go home every weekend, that's the big difference . . . if you go home every weekend you've never really left home.

This experience of school in Dunoon, complementing the direct influence of his father, gave John a lifelong respect for teachers and for the educational process.

> They were a very talented group of teachers. I think people at school learned enormously from the teachers. I don't know how fully teachers realise how important their function is. It's not simply the communication of knowledge or instruction of people in how to acquire knowledge for themselves or how to learn. There's a great deal of example involved as well and we were very fortunate, I think, to have teachers of such dedication, and such goodness as there were at Dunoon grammar school, certainly the time I was there.
>
> It didn't matter who you were, where you came from, what your income was, whatever, you all went to the school, got treated the same, you got a splendid education and you thanked everyone for the pleasure and privilege of being there and we carry that with us to this day.

As he recalled later of his Argyllshire education:

> I'm a great believer in what I call Scottish country schools. I think they are comprehensive, they are co-educational, they are relaxed, they are high-

65

class. I think they are splendid. I want to turn the whole of education in the world into the type of education I got.

I was brought up in a small Highland village with parents who were not particularly well off. My father was a primary school teacher and I had the most splendid education that it was possible to get. A millionaire could not have bought the education that I got in Ardrishaig Primary School, in Lochgilphead Secondary, in Dunoon Grammar School and in Glasgow University. I want everyone in Britain to get that quality of education.

His belief in education – and equality of opportunity as the best a community could offer to its young – never left him. But from the first days in senior school and university he found debating and politics his main preoccupations. A friend of his, Bob McLaughlan, recalled that:

At school he was a great debater, his quick and lively mind made rings round the rest of us, even then able to persuade by reason. I first met him when he was 14, newly arrived at Dunoon grammar school where I was also a pupil one year ahead. He often recalled my asking him on our first meeting 'Are you a socialist?' and when it turned out he was we were firm friends and became for long inseparable. I recruited him to the local Labour Party, where he delighted everyone with his charm, his spontaneous wit and his singing. I remember these songs, the first, a classroom song, was 'Scots Wha Hae', in a thin, pining voice from a round face. Even then he was the least materialist of people, little interested in money or possession.

John went to Glasgow University to study history. As he explained, 'You see, Scottish lawyers had this belief which they have now abandoned, but it was a good idea then that you should be given an arts degree first so you were educated before you were trained in the law.' But again at university debating and politics took over. By then the major political influences on his life – his belief in education, his sense of equality, his faith in the mutual support of community – were well established.

Returning to his school, Dunoon Grammar, and giving an interview after the 350th anniversary dinner in November 1991, he said:

I think perhaps we do now undervalue education in our society. I certainly think that we do undervalue the teaching profession. The teaching profession is the basic profession. There's not much point in having fancy doctors, fancy lawyers or indeed fancy university professors if you can't have a good teaching profession which not only helps to educate those who will be the sort of education élite of the future but manages to provide good education for all the people who come through.

JOHN SMITH'S SOCIALISM

CHRISTIANITY AND SOCIALISM

John's concern for opportunity and justice arose from quiet but profound religious convictions – convictions he held most strongly in the last six years of his life and which were perhaps best expressed in a speech he gave only 14 months before he died.

> The Second Commandment calls upon us to love our neighbours as ourselves. It does not expect human frailty to be capable of loving our neighbours more than ourselves: that would be a task of saintly dimension. But I do not believe we can truly follow that great Commandment unless we have a concept of concern for our fellow citizens which is reflected in the organisation of our society.

For John religion was a personal matter. But the more he progressed in his political life the more he felt his actions closely bound up with his Christian beliefs – the desire to help others, to strive for a better and more just society, to seek to improve people's lives and opportunities through the power of the community. In a little publicised interview to local church people in his own constituency in February 1990 he stated, 'I've always seen the gospel as being much concerned with social issues. After all, the command to love your neighbour means in my opinion the poor, old age pensioners, the struggling family, the people who are denied opportunity, usually through circumstances beyond their control. But it doesn't matter whether it was self-caused or externally caused. People need opportunity and I think that is what you should concern yourself with.' He set out his views when invited to deliver the annual R.H. Tawney Memorial Lecture in March 1993. Tawney was, in John's words, 'an uncompromising ethical socialist'. He was also a Christian.

> His Christian faith, which I am glad to share, was the foundation of his approach. But he did not claim – nor should any Christian – that Christianity could provide the only moral framework for an ethical approach to politics. Our own experiences tell us that an ethical approach to life and politics can be held as firmly by people of other faiths and by those who hold no religious conviction. Nor should Christian socialists ever seek to suggest that Christians must be socialists. Just because we, like Tawney, see our Christian faith as leading towards democratic socialist convictions, we must always recognize that fellow Christians might properly arrive at different conclusions from ourselves.
> Having established these caveats, let me assert my profound conviction that politics ought to be a moral activity and that we should never feel inhibited in stressing the moral basis of what we believe.
> But of course this is not all. We have to undertake the intellectual task of applying our moral principles in a way which results in practical benefit to our fellow citizens. And we must never be afraid of saying that we will

67

adopt a policy because it is, quite simply, the right thing to do.

Let us not underestimate the desire in our society, a desire which I believe is growing, for politics based on principle. And let us not deny the tide of opinion, which I believe is beginning to flow towards a recognition of the value of society and away from the destructive individualism of so much of modern Conservatism.[2]

John admired the writings of Archbishop William Temple, and was struck by Temple's three social principles which, he proposed, should guide our action – freedom, fellowship and service:

The theme that unites the writings of Tawney and Temple and which makes them so appealing to democratic socialists is their insistence on situating the individual in society. Individual freedom for them is only meaningful and achievable within society. This explanation of human experience is, of course, a core belief of democratic socialism. It provides an organising principle around which we believe our social order – both politically and economically – can and should be built. It is the way in which we believe individual freedom – our ultimate goal – can best be secured.[3]

John contrasted this approach with that of the political Right:

What I believe to be certain is that the flaws in the free market doctrines of the radical right are becoming more widely appreciated and more easily exposed than ever before. Their vision of humanity consists of individuals as decision-making units, concerned exclusively with their own self-interest, making transactions in a marketplace. It is a theory which makes very ambitious moral and economic claims; for example, that it alone preserves freedom and promotes prosperity. I believe, however, that it is a doctrine based on an absurd caricature of human behaviour, which grossly misunderstands the nature of freedom, and seriously ignores the value of society – even to the extent of denying its very existence.

The fundamental flaw in the individualism of the classical writers, and their modern counterparts in today's Conservative Party, is, I believe, their assumption that human beings conduct their lives on the basis of self-interested decisions taken in radical isolation from others. This thesis grotesquely ignores the intrinsically social nature of human beings and fails to recognize the capabilities that all people have to act in response to commitments and beliefs that clearly transcend any narrow calculation of personal advantage.[4]

The contrasting view of humans as essentially sociable beings, was, in John's view, a much more accurate observation of human behaviour and provided the basis for a more enduring politics:

The conclusion I reach is that the goal of individual freedom and the value of society, which we advocate as democratic socialists, is a theory of sustained intellectual force. When tested in the experience of humanity it can be found to be a better explanation of the lives and purposes of men and women than its rivals on the *laissez-faire* Right or the Marxist Left. We ought, therefore, in the battle for ideas which is at the centre of the political struggle, to be confident in the strength of our intellectual cause.

But I believe we must also argue for our cause on the basis of its moral foundation. It is a sense of revulsion at denied opportunity, injustice and poverty, whether at home or abroad, which impels people to work for a better world, to become, as in our case, democratic socialists. The powerful contribution of Christian socialists in all the denominations of the Church has always focused on the moral purpose of political action. How true it is that the Labour Party has owed more to Methodism than to Marx.

But it was that great Anglican, William Temple, who identified what he called 'the real wealth of human life', who saw that the individual was best fulfilled in the context of a strong community. That is the truth I want to re-assert today with confidence and conviction. That is why I believe the Labour Party must be bold in demonstrating our commitment to enhance and extend individual freedom by building a society which is dynamic and responsive to the aspirations of our people.[5]

Whilst holding firm religious beliefs, as a politician John was never dogmatic. He sought out practical solutions to problems. He judged every individual case on its merits. And he never lost sight of the ultimate political goal – improving the lives of people:

> Labour's goal must be about the advancement of individual people – about their freedom and their autonomy, about their ability to participate and their capacity to prosper – which we believe can only fully be achieved in the context of a strong and supportive society.

UNEMPLOYMENT

From the very first by-election of his political career – the 1961 North Fife by-election which he fought at the age of only 23 while still a University student – the waste and injustice of unemployment and poverty outraged John Smith. These concerns were the prime force of his political career. Often in private he would talk about his constituents, recounting, with anger, instances where deprivation and indignity had been imposed by unaccountable economic forces on individuals without means of redress. His maiden speech in the House of Commons in November 1970 was on poverty and the inadequacy of Tory measures purporting to redress it. As he described it, 'We are not impressed by the sincerity of the Government's desire to help the poor, in view of the small amount they are prepared to allocate, especially when we compare it with the large sums the Government have seen fit to dispense to other, much better-off sections of the population.'[6]

During the 1970s unemployment in Britain was to reach 1,204,400, but during the 1980s the Government's own unemployment total was to climb to 3,122,600 by July 1986. Indeed, from 1980 until John's death, unemployment in Britain was never to fall below three million men and women.

The theme of unemployment and its waste and indignity recurred most forcibly in one of his last great speeches – to the TUC Annual Congress in September 1993 – when he reaffirmed his faith in the goal of full employment. Only one Government had abandoned the 50-year-long commitment to full employment as a goal. And that was the Conservative Government of 1979:

> Next year will be the 50th anniversary of the 1944 White Paper on Employment. That White Paper said: 'The Government accept as one of their primary aims and responsibilities the maintenance of a high and stable level of employment.' Today I reaffirm that aim. The goal of full employment remains at the heart of Labour's vision for Britain.
>
> Labour's economic strategy will ensure that all instruments of macro-economic management, whether it concerns interest rates or the levels of borrowing, will be geared to sustained growth and rising employment. And that will be buttressed by vigorous supply-side policies to boost investment in the real economy, in our regions, in new technology and in the new skills upon which our capacity to create new wealth will depend. Labour's new economics recognises above all the value of people and the need for jobs. Jobs to create wealth; jobs to provide quality services; jobs to sustain a caring community. For there is no shortage of things that need to be done in our country today.

Unemployment, therefore, was never just an economic problem or a political tool with which to knock the Government, for John, who saw it as an evil both in terms of its impact on the individual and on society. First, unemployment was an appalling waste of individual potential. He spoke of the dignity of work and of the lost opportunities and unrealised talent that unemployment represented. And second, unemployment was, in his eyes, a shameful indictment of society as a whole. He believed it was the responsibility of a society to create opportunities for work for its citizens. By tolerating high levels of unemployment, society as a whole was failing in its moral duty to its people.

The horror and waste of unemployment was a theme to which he returned again and again in his speeches, no less so than when he spoke for Labour as Shadow Secretary of State for Employment. Then in debate after debate he berated the Government for its failure to tackle unemployment or even to take it seriously: 'the Government's policy is to brass it out . . . and to pretend that one can live comfortably and with a good conscience in a nation where there are nearly four million people unemployed.'[7]

John, for one, could not pass by on the other side. He was particularly disturbed by high levels of youth unemployment, angry at the waste of what he called 'this forgotten generation' and arguing that the country has a moral responsibility for them as individuals and as an essential investment for the future of the nation.

A speech he gave ten years ago reflected views he held throughout his political career and is worth recalling.

> We debate youth unemployment today because it is a crisis of national importance. Our young people are bearing the brunt of the Government's deflationary policies, which have caused unemployment to rise non-stop each year for the last four years. They are in danger of becoming a forgotten generation – denied the dignity of work, deprived of the training for skills, depressed by poverty and denuded of aspiration. We see them in all parts of the nation, but particularly in the hard-pressed industrial areas, kicking their heels disconsolately as one weary day of unemployment and lost opportunity follows another. If they are not so engaged, they are among the thousands of applicants for a handful of jobs when any enterprise advertises vacancies.
>
> Any manager in the engineering industry will say that if he looks, for example, for the recruitment of ten new apprentices – and they are a fast-disappearing phenomenon – he will receive hundreds of applications from youngsters bursting for opportunity, and well able to take advantage of it. With a heavy heart, he will have to turn away hundreds of ambitious and keen youngsters, and he and they will wonder – and so should we – what kind of society it is in which such things are permitted. Even for low-paid jobs with little by way of future opportunity, there are patient queues for the young unemployed.
>
> I will not dwell – I have no doubt that other Hon Members will – on the social consequences of mass unemployment among young people; on the effect on family life; on individual character; and on the very social fabric of the community. It is enough to assert that the lost opportunites for this forgotten generation must have a major claim not only on the attention of the nation but on its resources and its concept of moral responsibility, for we reject utterly any proposition that states that youth unemployment on this scale is either tolerable or inevitable.[8]

In March 1984, the unemployment figure had reached its highest level in history. At the same time, Britain had slipped into its first trade deficit in manufactured goods. During the Budget debate of that year, John, then Opposition spokesman on employment, homed in on these two points. He focused in particular on the number of long-term unemployed, which had reached more than one million, and expressed his fears for the young in particular, facing a future without work. He spoke with real anguish and foreboding about the social consequences of long-term unemployment. To tolerate such levels of unemployment, John felt, was deeply wrong.

> What will be the consequences for those young people as they grow older without work, and for those coming up behind them who face the same chilling prospect at the end of their formal education? Who is to say what the final social consequences will be on marriages and families which have been founded in the disillusioning and dispiriting framework of almost certain continuous unemployment? I do not know the final result. Indeed, which of us does? We know how adaptable is the human spirit, how socially stable are our communities, and how sturdy are our people. Perhaps those qualities will help the long-term unemployed, the young unemployed or others to weather their adversity better than we might be entitled to expect.
>
> The depression of the 1930s left its cruel mark on more than one generation. I believe that this self-induced depression must leave its mark too, in different ways. I know, too – indeed, I believe, and on behalf of the Labour Party I assert – that it is deeply wrong to tolerate such a level of unemployment in our society. We must quickly realise that it is our greatest social, economic and political problem.[9]

And John urged the Government to take action:

> I shall not be the only person to ask why the Chancellor did not accept the advice to embark on even a modest public works programme.
>
> The proposals are well understood by the nation. The Government have frequently been urged to do that by all sectors of industry, all parts of the nation and many parts of the political spectrum both within and outside the House. It is undeniable that our inner city infrastructure needs to be renewed. Our transport system needs to be modernised. The Victorian sewerage systems in many cities will collapse unless fairly urgent action is taken. The railways should be electrified. Much of our housing stock, especially in the public sectors, urgently requires modernisation. All those things have been neglected. One Victorian value that the Chancellor and his colleagues might seek with profit to emulate is the Victorian emphasis on proper public provision of certain essential services.
>
> Why are those urgent tasks to be so wilfully postponed? They are necessary, and if they are not carried out this year the need will be even more pressing next year and in the year after that. That those tasks will have to be undertaken is incontrovertible, and what is incomprehensible is that the Government should choose not to do them now, when they have unused resources on a massive scale and an army of unemployed who are desperate for work. Now is the time to match unmet needs with unused resources – in particular, unused human resources. Only the blind ideologues of the Government cannot see either the need for or the overwhelming desirability of a public works programme. I hope that the Secretary of State for

Employment urged that point upon the Chancellor. If he did not do so, he was neglecting his special responsibility to the unemployed. The absence of some such programme from the Budget and the public expenditure proposals is a national disgrace.[10]

This 'deep wrong', as he called it, would be a recurring theme in John's speeches throughout the Eighties and with renewed ferocity when he became Party Leader.

TRADE, ENERGY, EMPLOYMENT AND INDUSTRY, 1979–87

It was his commitment to the goal of full employment that made John argue not just for short-term remedial measures to get unemployed people back to work for a long-term expansion of the capacity of the economy. This led him to focus his attention on the new industry skills and the employment policy that Britain needed to rebuild its economy on a scale that would solve the unemployment problem.

I often sat next to John when he was Shadow Secretary of State for Trade and Industry. He made industry policy his subject in the mid-Eighties. For years, Labour industry policy had been caricatured as nothing more than nationalisation. John set out to show both how complex and how fruitful the relationship between industry and Government might be – a constructive partnership addressing the real needs of modern industry. This new partnership was neither corporatism nor *dirigisme*: it was Government and industry working to achieve together what neither side could be sure of achieving alone – the skills revolution, higher levels of investment, regional balance, technological advance and improved infrastructure.

This call for a new industry policy gained support not just inside the Labour Movement itself but throughout British industry. Even the CBI, traditionally no friend of Labour, came to acknowledge the importance of his analysis and proposed solutions and in November 1993 John, by now Leader of the Labour Party, was the main speaker at the CBI conference.

In February 1993, in addressing the Labour Local Government Conference, he set out to explain developing Labour thinking.

We should not be in favour of Government simply for its own sake. Equally we should not abdicate our responsibility to market forces. In the modern world, you simply cannot leave everything to the market any more than you can leave everything to the State. The political debate in Britain has been bedevilled for too long by simplistic arguments and false choices between these two extremes. The truth is that we need both dynamic markets and active Governments.

For years we have conducted a largely sterile debate about the ownership of industry and services as if privatisation and nationalisation

73

were the only conceivable choices in economic policy. In the Labour Party we see clearly the merits of the mixed economy and the need for an active and creative partnership between the public and private sectors.

We also comprehend that in a world of multinational ownership of companies, the only truly national asset we possess is the skills and accumulated knowledge of our own people. Ownership today is therefore largely irrelevant. As Neil Kinnock wisely observed, it is education and training that are the commanding heights of the modern economy.

Unfortunately these truths have simply not been understood by the Conservative Party. The mania about ownership has moved from Left to Right. The Tories' fixation is driving them to ever more absurd acts of privatisation – the railways, the post office, the coal mines, and the water of Scotland – all well beyond the limits of public approval and comprehension.

We know it is through the effective combination of dynamic markets and active Government that we can achieve both prosperity and social progress. What makes both work best is active citizenship. Markets need the stimulus of the empowered consumer; Government needs the stimulus of the participating electorate.[11]

John spoke on trade and energy in the Seventies, and on employment and industry in the early and mid-Eighties, before taking overall responsibility for economic policy as Shadow Chancellor from 1987. A recurrent theme during this period was the squandering of the revenues from North Sea oil paying for what he described as 'our standing army of unemployed'. As Junior Energy Minister and then Minister of State for Energy in the 1974 Wilson Government, John had overseen the development and regulation of the new North Sea oil fields, and alongside Secretary of State Tony Benn it was he who set up the British National Oil Corporation, the state company which owned 51 per cent of North Sea oil. Better than almost anyone, John knew what benefits would accrue to the British people in the years to come from the liquid gold of the North Sea.

In Opposition, he was deeply angry with what he saw as the waste of this precious revenue by the Conservatives – revenue which had been meticulously prepared for and anticipated by a Labour Government.

The true legacy which this Government inherited was North Sea oil revenue, which no previous Government had enjoyed. The Government did not work for, plan for, or earn those revenues. They were bequeathed a legacy which has amounted to £25 billion since 1979. Every year a Conservative Chancellor has been able to spend between £7 billion and £9 billion of North Sea oil revenues. Those revenues have had a desirable effect on the balance of payments and on the balance of trade, and their existence has masked the true effects of the deflationary policies of the Government on the balance of payments and the balance of trade. As the revenues of North Sea oil dwindle, those problems will become more starkly evident.

The revenues from North Sea oil are not the only benefit, but let us consider what the Government have done with their inheritance. They have not spent the revenue on re-equipping industry, retraining our people, improving the social infrastructure, giving us the best education system in Europe, improving housing stock, improving the Health Service or doing anything that a Government might reasonably be expected to have done with such a windfall. They have spent every penny piece on paying for the extra unemployment that they have created.

The Select Committee on Employment has calculated that every unemployed person costs the Government a minimum of between £5,000 and £6,000 a year in unemployment benefit, social security benefit, lost insurance contributions and lost value added tax. If one estimates the number of extra unemployed caused by the Government's policies at two million – a conservative estimate – the cost of supporting them must be £12 billion a year – far more than the annual revenue from the North Sea.

It was my good fortune to be a Minister at the Department of Energy before those revenues came in. At that time, work was being done to secure the developments which were subsequently of benefit to the present Government. I thought then that there would be a major argument about the use of North Sea oil revenues. I thought, perhaps naively, that the argument would be conducted on the traditional lines of dispute – that the Left, broadly speaking, would argue for the money to be used by the community in communal spending, regional policy development and the rest, while the Right, generally speaking, would argue for the money to be handed out in tax cuts to allow individuals rather than the community to make economic and political choices. If anyone had said in the years 1976 to 1978, when we began to think about North Sea oil revenues, that we would follow neither course but have a special plan by which we would save it all up to pay for the extra cost of unemployment that our policies would cause during the time in which we had North Sea oil revenues, he would not have been believed. It is unbelievable, and future historians will find it staggering.[12]

SHADOW CHANCELLOR

John took over as Shadow Chancellor in June 1987 when the illusory Tory mid-Eighties boom was moving towards its peak. But the gap between rich and poor was widening as never before. Within two years a Tory recession and mounting evidence of the impact of mass poverty were undeniable. But from 1987 onwards, John warned of two things: that the Tory stop-go economics were not underpinned by a solid record of industrial investment and that the obsession with top rate cuts for the very wealthy was neither fair nor economically efficient. Nigel Lawson's 1988 Budget handed out £6 billion in tax cuts. £4 billion of these went to the top five per cent. £2 billion went to the top one per cent.

John's swift analysis and prompt demolition of this now generally reviled Budget must stand as one of his finest Parliamentary achievements. His sense of fairness and justice was outraged. Moreover, he detected misgivings even then on the Tory benches, and warned that this budget might be their fatal mistake: 'a budget too far'.

John launched his attack with carefully chosen words of condemnation:

> The Budget which was presented to the House yesterday is an outrage. It is immoral, wrong, foolish, divisive and corrupting. As its full import began to sink in towards the end of the Chancellor's statement yesterday, I looked across at Conservative Members. A significant number did not wave their Order Papers or cheer the Chancellor on. Quite a number looked askance or troubled, and a few even looked concerned because they knew that what was happening was not right.
>
> Let us never forget that, in a country where there are still millions of people, young and old, thrown on the scrap heap of unemployment, where our Health Service is on the edge of collapse and where we have a growing underclass living in ever deepening drabness and despair, it is not right to slash the rates of tax for the highest paid and redistribute the tax collected to the tune of £2 billion and give it all – every penny piece – to those whose earnings and wealth have already been ostentatiously increased in recent years. No Budget in this century has more savagely redistributed the proceeds of taxation towards the super-rich. There is a simple rule about this Budget: the more you earn, the more you gain; the more you have, the more will be given unto you.
>
> A married man who earns £200,000 a year – not a fanciful figure in modern Britain – gains £33,314, over £640 each week. That is enough, I remind Conservative Members, to keep open the hospital ward in Wales which the Queen Mother opened and which is now closing because of the shortage of funds.[13]

As he proceeded with his demolition of the Budget, discomfort of Conservatives on the benches opposite increased.

> For a person on family credit in receipt of housing benefit and receiving £100 a week, the two pence cut in the tax rate will mean a gain of two pence a week or £1.04 throughout the year. I observe in passing that their poverty does not mean that they do not pay the huge increases in indirect taxes which are the hallmark of the Government's tax policies. So many of those who are facing the greatest difficulties get no help from the Budget.
>
> If we look to the higher ranges, the beneficiaries soon become apparent. The married man on five times average earnings, a salary of £64,000, will save £129 each week from this Budget alone – more than will be provided in income support for five people under 25 when the new social security system is implemented. For that same man on five times average earnings,

the reduction in his income tax since 1979 amounts to £81 weekly – more than the total income tax rate for two married couples, each with three children. The top ten per cent of households in Britain get 50 per cent of the concessions provided by the Chancellor. The bottom 50 per cent get only ten per cent of the gains.[14]

And in his peroration, John touched on the themes that would later underpin his approach both as Shadow Chancellor and then as Leader of the Opposition – fairness, justice, morality. He measured the budget against those standards and found it wanting.

> As we look through the Budget, we find that what is constructed behind a façade of tax reform is a major redistribution of income and wealth through the tax system. The Government took £2,000 million that could have been spent on the Health Service and gave it to the rich. That is why at its core there is a fault in this Budget, a moral fault. It is a massive political miscalculation. The Chancellor has revealed in all its vulgarity and unfairness the Thatcher vision of society, in which unfairness, inequality and injustice march side by side. The decent majority will react to what they have seen in the Budget. It is a Budget too far. It is the beginning of the end of Thatcherism.[15]

Even the supremely confident Chancellor Lawson was stung by this condemnation.

John's attack on the crudity and futility of Tory market dogma extended far beyond his immediate response to the 1988 Budget. He saw it as his role to expose the simplistic nonsense of 'trickle down economics'. Tax cuts for the very rich, John argued, would not necessarily revive industrial investment nor bring wealth flowing into the coffers of charities. And the reduction of public services necessary to achieve these tax cuts was harmful not only to the poor but to the security and well being of large sections of the population and the efficient functioning of the economy.

The public expenditure debate of 9 February 1989 marked John's return to politics after the massive heart attack he suffered in the autumn of the previous years. Anyone anxious about John's return to form was left in no doubt after his performance on that day. His speech included all the elements that made him stand out on the floor of the House – wit, incisiveness, mockery of the opposition, clever use of interventions, and the construction of a strong, detailed case in the best legal tradition.

He started off by thanking MPs for their good wishes and encouragement during his illness. With a characteristic glint in his eye, he took a gentle swipe at his opposite number, Nigel Lawson – a man of substantial girth. (John himself had lost two stone during his convalescence and looked leaner and fitter than most MPs in the Chamber.)

> Returning to these debates, I am struck by how little has changed. The Chancellor certainly has not changed. He is as bulky as ever, even if things have changed a little on this side of the Dispatch Box. The balance of payments deficit is worse. Interest rates are even higher, causing, as a direct result of Government action, savage increases in mortgage payments which have wiped out for several million, by a factor of several times, any tax benefits which they got from last year's Budget.[16]

He went on to attack the Government's 'deep-seated prejudice against public expenditure', whatever the economic circumstances. John argued that public expenditure was a crucial part of social development and economic expansion. John liked nothing more than to use the Government's own publications to prove his case and to undermine his opponents. This time it was the Public Expenditure White Paper itself. He brandished the document, taunting the then Chief Secretary John Major with it:

> In a new departure, perhaps even a breakthrough in the Government's presentation of facts, the Treasury has published a chart on page 17 of the White Paper relating to the Department of Transport, which analyses the road maintenance condition between 1977 and 1987. The chart usefully plots the progress of maintenance for local and national roads. It shows a sharp improvement in the maintenance standards achieved for both sectors until just after 1979, followed by a dramatic decline thereafter.
>
> Most helpful of all, the chart is bisected by a line; above the line it is marked 'better' and below the line it is marked 'worse'. I am happy to confirm that, according to the Government's own document, published as part of the White Paper on Public Expenditure, we see that road maintenance was constantly above the line during the period of the Labour Government and almost always below it during the time of the Conservative Government. If we are in any doubt about its meaning, the chart helpfully says 'better' on the top and 'worse' at the bottom.
>
> I am sure that is what the Chief Secretary had in mind when he said he loved to read these documents when he was trying to get to sleep. I recommend, if he is dozing tonight and finding it a little bit difficult to drop off, that he looks at charts showing the better and worse positions.[17]

John went on to argue for public investment and warned of the dire consequences of its neglect:

> I hope that the Government will understand this point, if none other made during the debate – that under-investment in the public sector harms the supply side of the economy. In the next decade, the country will face enormous challenges. After 1992, it will have to compete successfully with other countries in Europe for the single market, and with the rest of the world, including Japan, for the global market place, in which our industries must thrive and survive.

If we are to pay our way in the world and live within our means – we hear little about this from the Government – we must tackle the huge £14,000 million balance of payments deficit that is the result of Government policies, which is the major economic obstacle facing this nation in the years ahead. We must ensure that we are equipped to supply the demands for the domestic and overseas markets. If we are to enjoy a genuine supply side miracle, that will need public investment. We must invest in education and training, in research and development, and in the regions – using public resources where the market has failed to provide adequate investment, and where Tory claims of success are absurd.

I note that the Chief Secretary, both in his documents and in his speeches, refers occasionally to priority areas. I assume that, by implication, the other areas do not receive priority. The Right Hon Gentleman never refers to education and training, to research and development, or to regional development as priority areas. That is because they are all classified as non-priority areas, in terms of the Government's record and of their current viewpoint.

Education and training are the most important priority of all. Investment in education enhances the nation's most precious resource – the knowledge and skills of our people. From the nursery to the university, our country is failing to invest. It is one of the meanest providers of pre-school education for the under-fives, and there is inadequate provision all the way through secondary and tertiary education.

Research and development, skills training, regional development, the Health Service, overseas aid – all of these crucial areas were, John said, suffering from the Government's misguided antipathy towards public spending under any circumstances.

He ended his speech with an angry flourish that left no-one in any doubt – John Smith was back.

An analysis of the White Paper in terms of concept, and a scrutiny in terms of detail, reveal that the Government are trapped in a dogmatic obsession on public expenditure which undermines our national economic effort and impairs our quality of life. In terms of overseas aid, it also undermines our international reputation.

Nor is that the only evidence of the Government's wrong-headed approach and mis-shapen priorities. They are a Government who lavish benefits upon the rich but freeze child benefit and humiliate pensioners with the social security and housing benefits of last year. They are a Government whose notions of equity are revealed by their determination to press on with the poll tax – a form of taxation that every other civilised country has rejected. They are a Government whose sense of responsibility for national assets is revealed by the irresponsible privatisation of vital public services such as electricity and water. In other words, they are a Government whose policies do not remotely reflect the priorities that the nation needs. Sadly, the

White Paper reflects this Government's inadequate values, false priorities, and deceptive techniques, and it is not worthy of our support.[18]

By 1989 inflation was growing, the trade deficit worsening, and early signs of the oncoming recession were appearing. Conservative economic policy was starting to fall apart. There had been no permanent transformation of the British economy. The 'economic miracle' was nothing more than a phase in the familiar stop-go cycle, an unsustainable boom to be followed by an unavoidable recession.

An early sign of this failure appeared in the form of disagreement between Chancellor Lawson and 10 Downing Street over economic policy. The conflict was brought to a head by the continued and public interventions in policy by Sir Alan Walters from his position as the PM's personal economic adviser. Walters was a fierce critic of fixed exchange rates, and opposed Britain's entry into the Exchange Rate Mechanism of the European Monetary System. Lawson was in favour of the ERM. When it was announced that Sir Alan was to return from the United States to rejoin the Prime Minister's team as her personal economic adviser, it became increasingly clear that there was a serious rift between Numbers 10 and 11 Downing Street over exchange rate policy.

John was quick to exploit this rift. No-one who was in the Chamber of the House of Commons on 7 June 1989 will forget John's recital of the theme tune of *Neighbours*, the popular Australian sit-com, to poke fun at the Prime Minister and her Chancellor. He referred to a newspaper interview in which Mrs Thatcher had described Lawson as 'a very good neighbour of mine'. This was John's cue.

> Good neighbourliness is highly relevant to the confusion and disarray which lies at the heart of Government policy, and, on that subject, my sympathies are, to some extent, with the Chancellor of the Exchequer. After all, when he picks up the telephone and wants to get through to Number 10, it must be rather disconcerting to be told, 'Walters here. Would you like to speak to Griffiths?' [Professor Brian Griffiths – another adviser to the PM] It is not clear who the real Chancellor of the Exchequer is. We have here the nominal Chancellor for the Exchequer.
>
> Although he and the Prime Minister are neighbours, he should take account, as many of us who are aficionados do, of the theme song of the *Neighbours* programme, which we hear twice a day on BBC Television. The song goes:
> Neighbours – everybody needs good neighbours.
> Just a friendly wave each morning helps to make a better day.
> Neighbours need to get to know each other.
> Next door is only a footstep away.
> Neighbours – everybody needs good neighbours.
> With a little understanding, you can find a perfect blend.

Neighbours should be there for one another.
That's when good neighbours become good friends.[19]

John recited the entire verse to the delight of his own benches whilst the Chancellor sat red-faced and furious across the floor. Having tapped this sensitive vein of disagreement, John would not let it go. At every opportunity he asked, 'Who is running the economy? The Prime Minister or the Chancellor?' And each time, the beleaguered Chancellor became angrier and more discomfited.

Whilst providing marvellous material for John to joke about, the matter had very serious implications. The personality clash and power struggle between the PM and her Chancellor affected the whole direction of the Government's economic policy. And whilst there was uncertainty surrounding that policy, the pound would continue to suffer at the hand of jittery currency dealers in the City.

By October, the tension between Numbers 10 and 11 Downing Street was undeniable, and Alan Walters made no attempt to disguise his disagreement with Nigel Lawson. In a debate on economic policy on 24 October, John once again exploited the Chancellor's difficulties, mercilessly taunting Lawson:

> He knows how, month after month, the unelected and unappointed alternative Chancellor in Number 10 has thwarted his policies and contradicted his purposes – sometimes an allegedly indiscreet remark, sometimes a word in a City dining-room, and on occasion even a friendly reference to the need of the Chancellor to move on to other things.
>
> These are not the antics of some eccentric outsider; they are the work of a specially appointed insider in Number 10. When assessing this happy bond between Numbers 10 and 11 Downing Street, one extracts the true flavour of the team approach and a proper understanding of why no one in his right mind will believe that a team approach to anything is ever possible under the present Prime Minister. Isolated in Europe, isolated in the Commonwealth, at home she is increasingly isolated by the deference and lack of courage of a Cabinet who dare not challenge her overwhelming pretensions . . .
>
> I used to feel sorry for the Chancellor of the Exchequer, but it is time that he did something for himself. It is time for enterprise and individual responsibility. It is time that he told the Prime Minister that the moment has come to end the confusion and disarray in the formulation and explanation of Government economic policy. It is time that he said, 'Either back me or sack me.'[20]

On this occasion, John was more effective than he expected. His jibes were finally too much for Lawson. Stung by his public humiliation, and to the surprise of everyone including the Prime Minister herself, Lawson resigned later in the same week. This dramatic turn of events served to enhance John's reputation as a parliamentary performer.

In a speech to the House in July 1991, he underlined the economic significance of the political argument within the Conservative Party and set out an alternative economic strategy with its emphasis on supply side measures:

Hon Members know from their own experience that hardly a day goes by but someone, whether it is an industrialist, a businessman, a trade unionist or a teacher, tells us what he or she knows to be true: that our training is wholly inadequate to meet the needs of a modern economy and an ambitious society. Nearly every international comparison shows, with frightening repetition, that we are not only behind the rest of the European Community, but we seem so complacent that further slipping behind is inevitable. The Government have still not restored the resources available to their previous inadequate levels. They still do not appear to accept that they have a responsibility to foster training among the employed workforce as well as for the unemployed and young people. The Government say that they have no responsibility for helping to train the existing work force. Could anything be more foolish? They need urgently to revise their assessment because the other countries in the European Community do not hesitate to invest in such training. Investment in people, technology and the regions is the key.

In the 1990s in post-ERM Britain the economic agenda needs to be principally concerned with improvement in our supply side. Improving our productivity capacity and performance through investment will enable us to reduce the productivity gap between our country and our more successful competitors. It is through investment that we can create the wealth which alone can sustain higher living standards for our people and provide proper resources for our essential public services.

I say with genuine regret that that priority was absent in the locust years of the 1980s. We wasted the opportunities that were presented by North Sea oil revenue. We consumed instead of investing. The House will recall that demand was stimulated by a credit free-for-all and by tax cuts for the rich. Year after year, as we went from bust to boom to bust again, crucial investment in the infrastructure, the transport system, the public services and in training and manufacturing industry was persistently neglected.

We cannot afford to make those mistakes again in the pivotal decade that lies ahead. That is why, under a Labour Government, the thrust of fiscal and monetary policy will be to create the economic conditions that will maximise investment in our productive economy. We shall aim, as the Government failed to do, at macro-economic stability instead of practising the rollercoaster economics of boom and bust. [Interruption] Conservative Members do not like to hear that. Not only they but the public will hear it between now and the next general election.

We will promote a supply-side strategy that will improve the capacity of our industry and the skills of our people. Above all, ours will be a strategy for the long-term sustained recovery of our economy. Compare that, as the pubilic will do in the months ahead, with the wing-and-prayer antics of a beleaguered Government desperately seeking to create the illusion of recovery, no matter how insubstantial and – to borrow a phrase from the Chancellor – however shallow and short-lived.[21]

LEADER, 1992–94

When John became Leader of the Labour Party, his responsibilities broadened and the scope for the deployment of his parliamentary talents increased accordingly. Among his many concerns were standards in public life under a Government that had been in power too long. This concern allowed him to return to fundamental issues of democracy and accountability in public life. Another was Britain's future in Europe. And throughout the period his most passionate theme of all was his call for social justice.

But John could not ignore the economic agenda, because it was on this ground that the battle for social justice would be fought. National economic decline under the Tories became John's main theme, which he hammered home in his early speeches as Leader. Jobs, investment, training, the minimum wage and employment rights – these were the issues on which he focused his arguments. The other themes that mattered to him would have to come later.

He had an early opportunity to demonstrate his newly won authority in the House of Commons just two months after his election as Leader of the Party. On 16 September 1992, later to be known as 'Black Wednesday', Britain was forced out of the ERM and the Government spent millions of pounds of the national reserves trying to prop up the pound before its ignominious exit from the system. Government economic policy was in tatters. Labour called for an emergency debate in Parliament on 24 September. It cut short many MPs' holidays and interrupted preparations for the Labour Party's annual conference a week later.

This was John's first appearance in the Chamber of the House of Commons as Leader. MPs on all sides were keen to see how he would perform, whilst for many people outside Parliament, it was their first opportunity to assess the new Leader of the Opposition after its defeat in the general election.

John launched into an attack on the Government's mishandling of sterling in the ERM:

> The British people deserve to be told what went wrong. The Prime Minister had the responsibility to tell Parliament and the public today. We heard what he had to say – a few desultory remarks about economic policy, and a long rambling piece of nonsense about the future of the European Community.

As the Prime Minister was unable or unwilling to tell the House what happened, let us examine the facts. The genesis of the crisis was that Tory election promises of immediate economic recovery following the general election turned out to be totally false. Since April, all the main economic indicators of the real economy have deteriorated. Markets, consumers and industry increasingly lost confidence in the bogus predictions of a recovery that seemed constantly to be postponed.

What did the Government do? Nothing – absolutely nothing. Even as bankruptcies mounted, home repossessions kept rising, and unemployment remorselessly increased, the Government did nothing – absolutely nothing.

The continued weakening of the British economy that I have just described coincided with the predictable pressures on currencies arising from the uncertainties of the French referendum and higher German interest rates. The position called for prompt and decisive action to initiate and co-ordinate a Community-wide response – [Laughter]. So, this is a matter for laughter. Those who hold the presidency of the European Community deride a Community-wide response even before they hear what any such response might be. I have come across few such revealing actions. The Prime Minister and the Chancellor of the Exchequer, on this day of all days when they are in the dock, are chuckling.

As I was saying, the position called for prompt and decisive action, for a programme of growth in the Community, for jobs, for investment and for an early reduction in interest rates across the whole of the Community. Britain, holding the presidency of the Community, was uniquely well placed to take such action, as we repeatedly proposed, but it did not.[22]

John's confidence in this debate was evident from the way in which he dealt with interventions from his opponents. MPs usually intervene to try to embarrass, or to knock speakers off their stride. John's quick thinking enabled him to turn questions round to his own advantage, making fun of the questioner in the process, so that Tory MPs often regretted their intervention.

Mr James Paice (Cambridgeshire, South-East): I am very grateful to the Right Hon and learned Gentleman. Will he tell the House what would be the cost of his recovery package; and what effect that would have on public borrowing and on the currency market?

Mr Smith: I did not think that point would be pursued by Conservative Members today. After they lost £1 billion in a hopeless attempt to prop up the currency, and with increasing unemployment costing the taxpayer £8,000 for every person unemployed, they have the sauce to ask us the cost of a recovery programme. I ask them what is the cost of a non-recovery programme?

Mrs Judith Chaplin (Newbury): As the Right Hon and learned Gentleman called for a slash in interest rates three days before Britain left the ERM, does that mean that tradition has been replaced by opportunism?

Mr Smith: I was waiting for someone to blame me for the devaluation last week. The Hon Lady has not disappointed me. Of all the charges that could have been laid against me and of all the comment that there has been in recent weeks, the argument that I have been undermining Sterling is the most far-fetched that I have ever heard.[23]

John ended his first speech to the House as Leader of Her Majesty's Opposition with an attack on the Prime Minister's competence, an attack which heightened Labour's spirits and left the Tories distinctly uneasy:

In the course of a few weeks the one policy with which the Prime Minister was uniquely and personally associated, the contribution to policy of which he appears to have been most proud, has been blown apart, and with it has gone for ever any claim by the Prime Minister or the party that he leads to economic competence. He is the devalued Prime Minister of a devalued Government.

As Leader of the Opposition John had the demanding task of delivering Labour's immediate response to the 1993 Budget. This is one of the most onerous duties of the Leader of the Opposition, a great test of authority and skill. Contrary to what most people think, the Opposition has no prior access to the Budget statement. Like everyone else in the country, the Labour Leaders hear it for the first time as it is presented to the House of Commons by the Chancellor, and must respond with no previous knowledge of the tax changes, no opportunity beforehand to assess its impact or to calculate its implications for different income groups or sectors of society. A prompt, indeed instantaneous response is required.

John of course had the advantage of his experience as Shadow Chancellor. Having listened to the Chancellor's address he leaped to his feet and began a fierce attack on the Government for breaking its election pledges and hitting the most vulnerable people in society with new taxes. And like the lawyer he was, he had the case for the prosecution ready:

Those who have listened to this debate will have been shocked beyond belief at the cynicism of the Conservative Party which went into the last general election as the party committed to low taxation. [*Hon Members: 'We have done that.'*] Conservative Members say that they have done that. Some innocents on the Conservative benches describe the Budget as a Budget of low taxation. Let me remind the House of what the Government said during the last election campaign – [Interruption]. I know that some Conservative Members do not want to hear this, but I think that the public do.

Let me start with VAT. On 28 January 1992, the Prime Minister said: 'There will be no VAT increase. Unlike the Labour Party, we have published our spending plans and there is no need . . . to raise VAT to meet them.' It's difficult to be more categoric than that. During the election campaign, the Conservative campaign guide stated – [*Interruption.*] I know that that is a matter for humour, but we are entitled to treat it seriously. The guide stated: 'Following a series of unfounded and irresponsible scares by the Labour Party, the Prime Minister has confirmed that the Government has no intention of raising VAT further.'

To get precisely to the point, during the election campaign, at a press conference, Mr Tony Bevins of *The Independent* asked the Prime Minister on 27 March 1993: 'Can you give the same pledge that Mrs Thatcher gave in 1987 that you will not extend the scope of VAT to children's shoes and clothing, gas, electricity, and food?' The Prime Minister replied: 'I've made the pledge in the past. I've made it clear. We have no need and no plans to extend the scope of VAT.'

I do not know how the Right Hon Gentleman can sit there as Prime Minister of a Government who are capable of deceit on such a scale. The Conservative Party went into the election and was pressed day after day about increases in VAT and still came back with the answer, 'Lies and scaremongering from the Labour Party. The Conservative Party wouldn't do anything like that.' Those people make pledges as though they matter not a whit.

It is not just a question of VAT – and I will consider the effect of the VAT increase. The Prime Minister knows perfectly well that commitments were made on national insurance as well. On 28 January 1992, the Prime Minister stated: 'I have no plans to raise the top rate of tax or the level of national insurance contributions.' However, the Government have proposed today a one penny increase in national insurance contributions. No doubt they will go to the country and say, 'We haven't increased income tax. We have marginally increased the 20p band.' People are not so foolish. They understand clearly that one penny on national insurance is, if anything, worse than one penny on income tax. Apart from anything else, it bites further down the scale. On tax on income and tax on spending, the Conservative Party has cynically and ruthlessly betrayed the pledges which it gave to the people of this country. It will not be forgiven for that.[24]

This attack by John marked the beginning of what was to become one of the Labour Party's most effective campaigns against the Government: its exposure of the Tory record on taxation.

The Conservative party used to say that VAT was all right because, after all, people could choose whether they bought the goods on which VAT was levied. Will it tell us now that people can choose whether to have gas or electricity in their houses? The Government must know perfectly well that throughout the land a 17.5 per cent increase in fuel bills will push many families who are just on the edge, wondering whether they will manage, to despair.

It is no good the Government saying that they will adjust income support levels. Millions of people in Britain are poor but do not qualify for income support and will be hit savagely by the 17.5 per cent increase in the basic cost of living. The Chancellor says, 'It is all right: I have extended the 20p band.' But what does the extension of his band amount to? This year it amounts to about 25p a week and at best in future years it will amount to £1. How will that help people to meet the extra bills that they will have to pay as a result of all the other tax increases and reductions in allowances? Indeed, taken together, the tax increases announced in this Budget must be one of the highest hikes ever.

Would the budget bring down unemployment? he demanded. Where were the measures to promote investment or to boost manufacturing? Would the budget halt 'the long, sad economic decline of Britain'? But it was the deceit and the injustice of the Government's tax policies that angered John most of all: 'The Conservative Party is a party without honour and without feeling.'

In an Opposition Day debate on Government economic and social policy two months later, John developed the same theme: the Tories had proved themselves to be the party which looked after the interests of the very rich. John spoke for the concerns of the average tax-payer:

> Now we see clearly what the Tory tax strategy is, as we can review the Tories' long period in office. During the 1980s, when they were flush with cash from North Sea oil, the biggest and best handouts went to the rich. When the Government have come unstuck in the 1990s, it is the lower-paid and ordinary taxpayers who pay the price of their incompetence. It is like the old Victorian value: 'It's the rich wot gets the pleasure, it's the poor wot gets the pain.'[25]

The focus of John's attack on this occasion was the Government's incompetence. It came at a time when the Government's unpopularity had plummeted to a new low. A by-election in Newbury the previous month had been a disaster for the Conservative Party. The voters of Newbury turned a Tory general election majority of 37,000 into a Liberal Democrat victory of 22,000. This was followed on 27 May by a Cabinet reshuffle in which Norman Lamont lost his job as Chancellor, but which did little to restore the Prime Minister's fortunes.

Even outside politics the country appeared to be in trouble. The Grand National a few weeks earlier had been abandoned after an administrative blunder, and the collapse of a sea-side hotel in Scarborough had provided a powerful image of decline for the tabloid press. John made the most of this fateful series of events. In his speech, he cited example after example of the calamities befalling the Major administration:

> Although the betrayal of election pledges is bitterly resented throughout the country, it is only one of the reasons for the contempt in which the Government are held. Since the general election, we have seen one catastrophe piled on another. Not even the most inventive or ruthless scaremongering among my honourable Friends would have had the audacity to allege that any Government could be so consistently incompetent, so hopelessly accident-prone and so foolishly inept.
>
> I select but a few of the Prime Minister's recent triumphs: the billions of pounds lost in the panic and fiasco of Black Wednesday; the grievous damage to our energy resources which the disastrous pit closure programme has inflicted upon the country; the shady double dealing in the Matrix Churchill affair; the hopelessly bungled scandal of the education tests; and the disaster waiting to happen in the privatisation of our railways.
>
> In response to the plummeting popularity of the administration itself, revealed at Newbury and in the shire county elections, we have the Prime Minister's botched reshuffle. If we were to offer that tale of events to the BBC light entertainment department as a script for a programme, I think that the producers of *Yes Minister* would have turned it down as hopelessly over the top. It might have even been too much for *Some Mothers Do 'Ave Them*.
>
> The tragedy for us all is that it is really happening – it is fact, not fiction. The man with the non-Midas touch is in charge. It is no wonder that we live in a country where the Grand National does not start and hotels fall into the sea.

The House was in uproar. The Labour benches gleefully waved their ballot papers, revelling in the Tories' humiliation. This was John at his best, scornfully mocking the government's failure, building his evidence up to a devastating punchline. Even a few on the Tory benches could not help but join in the laughter.

EUROPE

Debates concerning the Treaty of Maastricht provided John with another opportunity to spell out his deeply held belief that economic prosperity cannot be separated from social justice. Fairness and efficiency were, he argued, inextricably linked. Europe had to be a community – and not just a marketplace. A common market had to have a social dimension, hence his support for the Social Chapter. Growth to be sustained had, he argued, to be shared.

In the lengthy and tortuous passage of the Treaty of Maastricht through the British Parliament, the Labour Party called a debate on the Social Protocol of the Treaty. John Major had refused to sign the Social

Chapter of the Treaty, which had consequently to be removed from the body of the Treaty and attached as a Social Protocol which the other 11 member states of the European Community duly signed. The Labour Party opposed the Government's opt-out from the Social Chapter, and insisted on a vote on the issue before the European Communities (Amendment) Act – the result of the Treaty of Maastricht – could come into force.

The debate took place amid high tension because Tory Euro-rebels threatened to vote with the Opposition in order to defeat the Government. With his narrow majority, John Major's own position was in serious trouble.

John Smith argued that the Conservatives' opposition to the Social Chapter was absurd. For John, this was a simple matter of fairness and decency – in his own words, accepting a policy because it was right:

> I shall remind the House just what the Social Protocol is about. I do not make any enormous claims for its proposals, which are fairly modest. But the Government say that the proposals are a sinister threat to our economic future, a deadly plot by the Brussels bureaucrats to destroy jobs and economic growth from which, in the nick of time, our heroic Prime Minister has rescued us all. The irony of the Prime Minister posing as a job protector will not be lost on the millions of people who have been victims of the economic policies for which he has been responsible as Chancellor and Prime Minister. That self-styled saviour of jobs and growth has the worst record on jobs and growth of any British Prime Minister since the war.
>
> It is when one examines the provisions of the Social Protocol that the absurdity of the Government's claims is revealed. In what sense and in what way does the improvement of the working environment to protect workers' health and safety or the improvement of working conditions impede economic growth? How on earth can equality between men and women in labour market opportunities and treatment at work be considered economically harmful in a civilised, modern state?
>
> It becomes even more absurd when one appreciates that the purpose of the agreement is to have similar rights and opportunities in every Community country to create a level playing field of social opportunity. We hear much about level playing fields from Conservative Members who mention them nearly every day in the Chamber. It is odd that they will not adopt that concept in relation to the rights of working people, and men and women. That concept is fully understood by the rest of the Community, which is why all the other 11 member states readily agreed to the Social Charter of 1989 and the social action programme that flowed from it. It is why they have consistently resisted British Conservatives' attempts to prevent further progress in the social sphere. They agreed to the protocol because they all understand what the British Conservative Party is incapable of appreciating – that economic success and social progress go hand in hand.[26]

John used real life examples to illustrate his argument for social justice generally and in doing so to expose the double standards of the Government:

> I want to remind him [*the Prime Minister*] of the wages that are actually being paid in the Britain of which he is Prime Minister today. A 28-year-old care assistant working in a private nursing home works 60 hours for £1.33 an hour. A coach driver works 60 hours a week for £2.10 an hour. A forecourt attendant in a petrol station works 70 hours a week for £1.40 an hour. That is the philosophy of the Conservative Party and that is how it affects real people in the real world.
>
> How many Conservative Ministers would contemplate accepting those rates of pay for themselves or for their families? If it is not acceptable to them, why should it be thought acceptable for anyone else? What makes it even harder to stomach is the constant rise in salaries, pensions and perks for the highest-paid executives at the same time as the exploitation of vulnerable people proceeds and the Government walk away from their responsibilities to those people. It is that weird Tory double standard on incentives: poor people can be motivated only by the thought of even greater poverty, but the rich are to be inspired by the lure of even greater wealth.
>
> The Government's approach to international competition is just as crude. It is to compete against Taiwan on wages rather than against Germany on skills. The Government say that if our competitors pay low wages, we must follow them down. If there is no employment protection in countries against which we compete, such protection apparently cannot be afforded here either.
>
> We in the Labour Party believe that that approach is wholly flawed. Not only is it totally unjust to our people, it is not related in any way to the dynamics and realities of today's world economy. Investors at home and abroad today are seeking skills, technology and a highly motivated and self-confident work force.

In two highly dramatic votes at the end of that debate, the Opposition's amendment was narrowly defeated, but on the substantive motion the Government was also defeated. With the House in turmoil and the Prime Minister in serious trouble, the Government announced a confidence motion to take place in the Chamber early the next morning. John Major let it be known that if he lost that vote, he would seek the dissolution of Parliament, with a general election following. In his speech the following morning, John mocked the Prime Minister's threat of an election:

> It appears not to have occurred to the Prime Minister that his tactic of employing a quasi motion of confidence in Her Majesty's Government is not a sign of confidence but a display of weakness. The Prime Minister lost the argument in a House in which he has a clear overall majority on the most important aspect of his legislative programme – one which, moreover, he has

stamped with his own personal design and authority. As a result of his failure, he has been forced to make a humiliating threat to his own party: that unless Conservative Members come into the Government Lobby today he will press the self-destruct button of a general election, which both he and they know would result in a massive defeat for this Government and in the loss of their seats.

I noticed that one of the rebels said on radio or television this morning or yesterday that a general election would result in the loss of possibly one-third of the Conservative seats in this House of Commons – hardly a sign of confidence. It is hardly a symbol of authority to go to your own party and say, 'If I can't drag you into the Lobby, I'll give your electors a chance to get rid of you.' That is this man of confidence, this triumphant hero of the negotiating table, this self-confident leader of the Conservative Party. Former leaders of the Conservative Party will be turning in their graves when they think of what is being done in the name of the Conservative Party today.

Faced with the prospect of losing their seats, the Tory rebels stepped back in line and secured the Government's majority, saving John Major at least for a time. For John, in the debate over Europe, the Social Chapter epitomised the stark difference between Labour and the Conservatives:

> In any modern democracy, economic progress must be accompanied by enlightened working practices. Progress cannot happen without the willing participation and active endorsement of the people who operate the machines and build the roads and work the technology.
>
> The Labour Party agrees with our European partners that the primary resource of the Community, the single most important element in our wealth creation, is people – the working men and women of Europe. That is why we see the Social Chapter as an integral part of the Treaty of Maastricht, and that is why the development of common basic standards for people at work is central to our vision of a future Europe.
>
> Because Europe is not just a marketplace, it is a community. Because progress is not just about economics, it is about justice. And because a civilised society is measured not just by its wealth but by the treatment of its citizens.[27]

John was passionately in favour of Europe. He had never seen any difficulty in reconciling a sense of national pride with a desire for international co-operation. In 1971 he had gone so far as to vote against the official Labour whip in supporting European membership. John wanted Britain to be a leading player in Europe. He saw the potential for joint action to solve problems. Moreover he thought that both our economic strength and fairness could be advanced through European integration. Personally at ease with and a close friend of many European leaders, he was angry at the way the opportunity for action and for leadership was being wasted, for purely internal party reasons, by British Conservatives.

> Under the Conservatives, Britain's attitude to Europe has been confused, suspicious, reluctant and ambivalent. Instead of leading the way in the Community, Britain has trailed along behind whilst others have taken the lead. Instead of embracing the vision of shared prosperity and social justice, the Government rejected the case for employees' rights and fair wages. Instead of using the British presidency to initiate Europe-wide action to counter recession and to attack unemployment, Mr Major was engaged instead in word games about subsidiarity, a concept which he urged for the Community but resolutely denies in the United Kingdom. And instead of making Britain a leading power on the European stage, [he] believed we were sinking – through the staggering incompetence of this Government – into the economic second division of member states.
>
> This signal failure of leadership has minimised our influence over our EC partners, weakened our ability to steer the future direction of the Community, and severely reduced the benefits to our people that wholehearted participation in Europe would undoubtedly bring.

John Smith believed that strength in Europe would enable Britain to push for more co-operation on the world stage. He was convinced that far more could and should be done on the international level to change the world for the better. When John was Shadow Chancellor he paid visits to the IMF and the World Bank. His consistent themes were a call for measures for debt relief, reform of the UN and a shake-up at the IMF and World Bank. John continued to pursue these themes when he became Leader of the Party.

Soon after his election he was asked to head the Socialist International Committee on Economic Policy, Development and the Environment. This Committee was to draw up a report for Spring 1996 on a blueprint for the world economy and reform of international institutions. Work had begun on the project, including numerous meetings with John in the chair. He saw the potential for the Committee to set a new agenda and force the pace of change. John believed very firmly that much could be achieved through effective international co-operation, as long as the right mechanisms were in place. He set out his ideas most clearly to a meeting of the Socialist International in the Palais des Nations, Geneva, in February 1994, in which he criticised the two Bretton Woods institutions – the IMF and World Bank, and called for a radical reorganisation:

> The two institutions are increasingly doing the same job – and a major and consistent criticism is that both are doing the same job badly. Cynics in developing countries like to compare the two with a torturers' double act. The Fund does the nasty stuff and the Bank offers the tea and sympathy.

I believe that serious consideration should be given to merging the Fund and the Bank into a single institution and at the same time bringing the new organisation into a closer and more co-operative relationship with the UN specialised development agencies – such as the UN Development Programme, the World Food Programme and UNICEF. A combined Fund and Bank could be administratively leaner and, I hope, more effective in mobilising both resources and economic policy advice. I appreciate that such a proposal will send a shiver through Chevy Chase, Maclean and other Washington suburbs – but, after all, the army of economists that work for the Bank and the Fund are all experts on coping with structural adjustment.

Simply rearranging the structures of policy-making does not, of course, guarantee better policies. But I do believe that there could be positive gains from focusing the attention of the international community on a UN Economic Council which would gain greater status than that enjoyed by the current G7, and which would have clear authority over a restructured system of international financial institutions.

And he set out the principles that he believed should underpin modern economic policy – principles which lay at the heart of his economic vision for Britain but which were just as relevant to international economic co-operation.

For me, economic progress and social justice are intertwined and inseparable. That is why I want to see economic policies that encourage growth, employment and investment in people. It is an approach built on the idea that our most precious resources are the skills and talents of people. In the jargon of economic theory it is an investment in human capital. And it is an approach that I believe that is just as applicable to the most advanced industrial country as it is to the least developed country.

For how are modern industrial economies going to remain competitive and create jobs if they do not invest massively in training and the skills of their workforce – when all the evidence shows that higher levels of technology require greater flexibility in the workplace? And how are poor countries going to escape poverty if they do not invest in the health and education of their own people – when all the evidence shows that reduced rates of infant mortality and higher literacy rates are not merely inter-related but are the very foundations of development itself?

This is the agenda which we in the Socialist International can make our own. We stand for investment in people, for equal opportunities for men and women, and for the opportunity of work. For we want a people-centred economics in which markets must serve people and not the other way around. And we stand for partnership and co-operation at home and abroad. For we know that acting together we can do far more than any individual state.

This is the economic vision that I believe will shape the next century. In our meeting today I hope we can explore some of these ideas and begin to develop a new blueprint for the world economy. We should be bold and ambitious and follow the advice of George Bernard Shaw – 'some see things as they are and ask why – we should dream of things that never were and ask why not?'

John was fundamentally optimistic about what individuals working together – and politicians in particular – were capable of achieving, if only they set their minds to it:

Cynics will no doubt look for the pitfalls. But they will always find a host of reasons why change is impossible, even undesirable. Surely the lesson of history is that we must be grateful that the cynics were outnumbered by the people of vision back in 1944 when the principles of multilateralism and international co-operation were so successfully set in motion. Because it was these principles and the institutions that embodied them which generated an era of economic progress and prosperity never seen before.

For we are living at a time of great change. A time of enormous challenge and opportunity. It is this generation that must shape the new post-Cold War world. It is up to us to reforge the institutions of the international community. We are the architects of the 21st century – trying to build a world that will be more peaceful and more prosperous than ever before. And if we are to provide a blueprint for a better future, we must be ready to change and to think how things could be different. And instead of asking why, ask why not.

STANDARDS OF PUBLIC LIFE

John was very conscious of the responsibilities of public life, and he felt strongly about maintaining high standards in it. He hated dishonesty and deception, particularly by those who were in positions of authority over others. He detested the abuse of authority in whatever form. Worst of all he hated the hypocrisy of those who lectured to others about standards of behaviour but did not abide by the same standards themselves. He was in no sense a prudish man. He loved fun, he was not averse to raucous behaviour and he enjoyed outrageous jokes. But he never lost sight of his public position or of the responsibility that came with his authority. He set himself high standards and he expected the same of others.

He also believed in the intrinsic value of public service. He described this in a speech he made to the Royal Institute of Public Administration in 1991. It's title was 'The Public Service Ethos'.

After a decade in which public servants (be they teachers, nurses, health workers, carers, local government employees or civil servants) have been hounded and pilloried, it is time for a new commitment to the value, and values, of public service. The case for public welfare is that it not only provides the most effective means of meeting the needs of the majority at different periods of their lives, but also strengthens and unites the nation. An economy which is supported by a healthy and well-educated labour force will be able to compete more effectively with other advanced economies. A society which gives priority to welfare will not only be more just but also more cohesive, and therefore more socially and politically stable.

It follows that those who work for the public service deserve not blame but praise. They are engaged, not in some parasitical, illegitimate activity, but in an essential national task – serving the community. We need top calibre people to join and serve in the public service. We need to see they are properly trained and rewarded. And their work must be held in high esteem.

One aspect of our public life, which is in my opinion undernoticed and under-regarded, is the integrity with which it is conducted. I had myself experience, when a minister in the Department of Energy, of the allocation of extremely valuable licences for oil and gas exploration and development. The oil companies, who were applicants for these licences, universally confirmed to me that the UK was without peer in its freedom from any sort of corruption by politicians or officials. That integrity in our public life, which owes so much to the very high standards of personal conduct maintained by servants of our state, is a pearl beyond price. We should esteem it more highly and recognize it as a truly honourable achievement. A recognition of the importance of public services to the whole nation and of the value to the whole nation of those who provide and maintain them will be a guiding principle of the next Labour Government.[28]

John's arguments on these themes were given added force after a series of events which appeared to reflect a very serious decline in the standards of some politicians and senior civil servants. These included the payment of Norman Lamont's private legal fees out of public funds; the manner in which Michael Heseltine's pit closure plan was carried out; the Matrix Churchill trial and the sale of arms to Iraq; the BCCI fiasco; scandals in privatisation, contracting out and the appointment of quangos. And later came the Asil Nadir scandal, questions over Tory fundraising and the resignation of Michael Mates.

In January 1993 John decided to give a speech about standards in Government, their recent decline, the abuse of authority and the Government's failure to take responsibility for the consequences of its actions. Aware of the unease in the country at large and the general disillusionment with those who held positions of power, he sought to remind the country of what was expected from those in public service.

There was a time, not so long ago, when ministers resigned over events which left them seriously diminished in the eyes of the British people. In April 1982 Lord Carrington, then Foreign Secretary, resigned from the Government because his department had failed to anticipate the Argentine

95

invasion of the Falkland Islands. Mrs Thatcher spent a long time trying to persuade him to stay on. But, according to a *Times* report, the day after Lord Carrington's resignation, 'he felt that he had been head of the department responsible for the policy, the policy had failed and therefore it was a matter of honour that he should go'.

It was as simple as that. No ducking and weaving. No excuses. No long interviews on *Walden*. The policy had failed and therefore it was a matter of honour that he should go.

That's what people expect. They expect the Government to act in their best interests and when things go wrong they expect someone to take responsibility for it. But when did we last hear a member of this Cabinet mention the word 'honour'?

Somewhere along the line the concept of responsibility has been thrown overboard by this Government. And it has been replaced by a different code – survival. Survival by any means, at any cost, until the last possible moment.

This is a Government from which nobody resigns unless absolutely forced to do so by overwhelming pressure from the public, the media and their own backbenchers. They mislead parliament, they break the law, they jettison policies which once formed the cornerstone of their entire programme, they use public money to pay private legal bills, they are forced into retreat by the anger – the anger – of the British people, and nobody takes responsibility.

One is forced to ask the question: what on earth does it take for a minister to resign from this Government?

There can be little doubt that this attitude, this hanging on at all costs, is the hallmark of a party too long in power. But the arrogance of power that we are witnessing today has more serious manifestations. Lines have been crossed that leave decent people feeling uneasy and poorly governed.

It has become standard practice under this Government for Tory politicians to move from senior positions in the Cabinet to influential posts in privatised industries. It is even the case that ex-ministers accept directorships in industries for which they themselves established the regulatory environment.

Should former ministers be allowed to benefit in such a way from policies they themselves implemented when in the privileged position of Government? I think not. The too-close relationship that has developed between this Government and the private sector, and particularly those industries privatised by this Government, is unhealthy and improper.[29]

John blamed much of this on the arrogance of a Government too long in power and wanted to restore the former values. This important speech set the tone of his entire approach to public responsibility, and it struck a chord with people outside politics who looked on with alarm and disgust at the falling standards of some of their political leaders.

John was also concerned about the politicisation of top echelons of the Civil Service. He argued for a clearer definition of responsibilities of civil servants and duties in relation to Ministers, calling for 'protection in our system for a civil servant who correctly identifies a distinction between the national and a party interest, and who seeks to resist the pressure to cross that line'. But he also called for constitutional change to prevent abuse of power by any individual or party.

> The over-centralisation of British Government which has gone on apace over the last decade seriously accentuates the problem in our country, with too few checks and balances against the arbitrary use of power. We need to strengthen the power of parliament over the Executive. We need to devolve power to the nations and regions of Britain. We need to revive and restore local government as a vibrant part of our democracy.
>
> It is also clear to me that the individual in Britain has too few rights in relation to the state – or indeed as against the abuse of private power. A first step should be the enactment of a Bill of Rights to protect and defend the individual. We also need a Freedom of Information Act which gives us all – the sovereign citizens of this country – the right to know what Government knows and what it does on our behalf.
>
> And the overriding precept must be openness. The mature democracy towards which we must strive will be a democracy in which there is wide participation, keen debate and open decision-making. It is ultimately the only way to ensure accountable and responsive Government.
>
> To conclude, let me return to my office correspondence. Although the outrage expressed in so many of these letters makes depressing reading, the strength of feeling and prevailing sense of morality and fair play they convey has impressed me greatly. I would like to think that we are, to borrow the words of Woodrow Wilson, witnessing a renaissance of public spirit. Perhaps it has taken the recent catalogue of events of which I have spoken this evening to rouse the nation's indignation, and this will indeed prove a catalyst for change.
>
> I hope so. It is certainly my intention to campaign for that change; to assert the rights of ordinary people to hold their Government to account; and to start to fashion a new constitution for a new century.

John developed this theme of constitutional change in many subsequent speeches. He saw democratic renewal as central to his vision of a future Britain, an important element of a John Smith Government. A key speech was 'A Citizen's Democracy' in which he set out his plans for constitutional reform and democratic renewal.

> I have no hesitation in saying there is an undeniable and pressing need for constitutional reform in this country. Undeniable because – as I hope to demonstrate – our structures and institutions are clearly failing properly to represent the people they were set in place to serve. And pressing because of the mounting sense of disenchantment and cynicism amongst the people of

this country about our political system, a deeply disturbing trend that must be checked if we are to secure the future health of our democracy.

I am arguing for a new constitutional settlement, a new deal between the people and the state that puts the citizen centre stage. A deal that gives people new powers and a stronger voice in the affairs of the nation. And a deal that restores a sense of cohesion and vitality to our national life.

I want to see a fundamental shift in the balance of power between the citizen and the state – a shift away from an overpowering state to a citizens' democracy where people have rights and powers and where they are served by accountable and responsive Government.

It used to be said that the subject of constitutional reform was of interest to no-one but the so-called chattering classes. Critics considered it a distraction from the bread and butter issues that matter to most voters. But in this atmosphere of decline and gloom, it is abundantly clear that people across the nation do care deeply about the way they are governed, and they feel angry and frustrated with a system that isn't working.[30]

John was a keen advocate of devolution for Scotland and Wales and of the decentralisation of power in the form of re-invigorated local government. He also favoured the abolition of the hereditary principle of the House of Lords. He wished to see easier access to justice. And he argued for individual rights to be strengthened, by a Bill of Rights, a Freedom of Information Act and a Charter of Employment Rights. John, often portrayed as staid and traditional, was actually a proponent of radical constitutional change:

We live in an elected dictatorship, in which the centralisation of power suffocates debate and dissent. In which the rights of people and communities are disregarded on a daily basis. In which the accountability of democratic election is continually displaced by the imposition of new agencies from central government, answerable to no-one but themselves and their masters.

Since 1979 there has been a systematic and sustained attack on the whole concept of local government as the Conservatives, under a mis-shapen appreciation both of the role of government and of the rights of people, turned their back on their party's once proud municipal commitment.

They misunderstand their own history almost as much as they blight our future. For it is a vital part of the plurality of our governance that local communities should have powers of initiative and links of responsibility which only effective local government can create.

I look forward with keen anticipation to creating a new and creative partnership with local government – a partnership of achievement which will refresh the roots of our democracy.

I look forward with a similar sense of commitment to devolving power from Whitehall to the nations and regions of Britain. So that we can create a truly modern state, in which power – real power – comes closer to the people. And choices – real and differing choices – can be made according to the needs and aspirations of all parts of the kingdom.

And I look forward to the enactment of a Bill of Rights; to abolishing the bizarre hereditary basis of the House of Lords; and to giving the people themselves the choice on how they elect their representatives in the House of Commons.

We see the reform of the British constitution – a vital task for the next Labour Government – set clearly in the context of our strong and continuing commitment to a democratic and successful European Union. Indeed our reforms will enable new and exciting links to be created between all levels of government in Britain and their counterparts in our partner nations.

Our vision of Europe combines economic achievement with social progress: it also requires the extension of democratic control so that the new Europe we build is firmly based on the consent of its people.

But it is not enough to reform the institutions of government: we must also make vital changes to its manner and style. Central government in Britain is disfigured by obsessive secrecy, by concealment and manipulation of information, and by an ingrained aversion to open debate. These features are, of course, accentuated when we have Ministers to whom they are all too useful tools.

But the weasel words of evasion which are littered through the evidence before the Scott Inquiry are part of an unhappy culture as well as the product of Ministerial intrigue.

We need a Freedom of Information Act which will make available to the people of this country the facts about how their nation is governed, facts which are crucial to informed democratic decision making by people as well as legislators.

The next Labour Government will be a reforming Government, carrying through major changes to make our Government more efficient and democratic; more purposeful and more participative. And in that spirit, I intend to lead an administration which will be proud to be open and accountable for its actions to the people it serves.[31]

Giving the Charter '88 lecture, as Leader of the Labour Party on 1 March 1993, he had stated:

I am arguing for a new constitutional settlement, a new deal between the people and the state that puts the citizen centre stage. A deal that gives people new powers and a stronger voice in the affairs of the nation. And a deal that restores a sense of cohesion and vitality to our national life.

These were sentiments which John had already been articulating for decades when Prime Minister Jim Callaghan had specifically chosen him to pilot the Labour Government's crucial Devolution Bill through the House of Commons in 1976.

Though initially lukewarm on devolution, John came to be its principal advocate. And when appointed to head the Government's devolution team John set about his task with characteristic diligence, carefully constructing a powerful case for the proposals he advocated. In the highly charged atmosphere in Scotland at the time, he had to steer a path between two hostile sets of opponents.

As he described it, 'Those who argue that we should maintain the status quo take refuge in the comfort of familiarity. A policy of "no change" is no doubt comforting and familiar, but I think it ignores the defects of the present system and the change in the climate of opinion in Scotland. At the other extreme, a vociferous minority of Scots argue that the only future for Scotland is complete independence.'[32]

Characteristically, John's own approach rejected these two extremes, and were developed on the basis of a recognition of existing circumstances and future needs.

John had little time for the arguments of the separatists. Speaking to the Political Studies Association Work Group on UK Politics at the University of Strathclyde on 13 September 1976, he outlined his approach on the basis of first principles. He started by acknowledging both the circumstances of the present and the need for change for the future:

> The United Kingdom, by comparison with many modern states, is geographically small. Communication between most parts of it is now usually, if not cheap, at least efficient. The intermingling of population through migration from one area to another, especially since the industrial revolution, the more recent growth of large national and international companies with branches in all or many parts of the country, the influence of the media, the national press and radio and television – and the steady accretion of powers to central government over the past century and a half, have all conduced to the unity of the state. More recently however there has developed pressure for the governmental power to be spread from the centre outwards. Sometimes this has taken the form of a demand of administrative decentralisation, namely moving the locus of decision making away from London to other creatures. Sometimes it has expressed itself as a demand for greater control by those living and working in particular areas of the country over the decisions that affect their life at home and on the job . . . I believe this is a healthy development to which Governments should seek to respond. Just as we should be alert to make policy changes reflecting Britain's changing role in the world, so should we be prepared to make a reforming analysis of how we govern ourselves in our own country.
>
> In making such an effort we must relate our reforms to the practical realities of life in this country – to its closely knit structure as well as to the desire to move power outwards from the centre, to the history of our institutions as well as our expectations from them in future.

And having established the case for change, John then rejected what he saw as the blinkered approach of the Scottish separatists.

I need not rehearse the problems of turning the clock back to before 1707 and attempting to recreate a separate independent state in the last quarter of the 20th century. Britain as a Union – not Scotland, not England, not Wales – has been by any reckoning among the most successful political units in history. To break it up now – after the close interconnections which have been forged not only in economic organisations but also in shared political and social assumptions – would to my mind be an act of spectacular folly. Not for one moment do I believe that it is the wish of the Scottish people to acquire a separate navy, army and airforce or the privilege of sitting in the United Nations between Saudi Arabia and Senegal.

Yet John's advocacy of Labour's devolution proposals came not only from careful intellectual analysis. It was built on the solid bedrock of his deep pride in Scotland and his own Scottishness. He therefore could justify in personal and compelling terms how he reached his position.

I say this not just because every opinion poll taken in Scotland indicates an aversion to separatism. I say it as a Scot myself, representing a Scottish constituency, born and brought up in Scotland, living and wishing to continue living in Scotland, a member of a Scottish profession, with children at Scottish schools, and having roots too deep in Scotland ever to wish too sever them. I think that I am as entitled as any separatist to speak for my fellow countrymen. While they certainly wish to see a Scottish dimension in Government and wish a full recognition to be made of Scotland's past, present and future contribution to the Union, they even more wish to be and remain British.

CONCLUSION

Throughout his 24-year parliamentary career John covered in his speeches many issues within many departmental briefs. But underlying almost all his public utterances was a recurring theme of opportunity: opportunity for people to advance by education; opportunity for people to realise their potential to the full; opportunity for everyone to participate in the democratic process.

John spoke out against the 1988 Budget, the indignity of the Poll Tax, the abolition of minimum wages, the refusal to endorse the Social Chapter and the appalling waste of mass unemployment. He set up a social justice commission to devise new policies for the welfare state. He believed in trade unions as an effective defender of employees' interests – a sword of justice for decent conditions and fair wages – and argued that the case for strong trade unions was as compelling now as it was at first or has ever been in the history of our country, not least because of the exploitation and abuse now taking place in workplaces throughout Britain as minimum wages and standards are abolished.

Even in what was to be the last week of his life, he worked furiously in Parliament to try to secure decency and fairness for disabled people while the Government sought, by the unfairest of means, to destroy a Private Member's Bill that would have helped six million men and women.

It was typical of him. John's politics were not born out of envy, but from a strong desire that everyone should have a fair chance in life. John Smith was an extraordinary man who never thought of himself as anything other than ordinary, and he wanted for ordinary people all the opportunities that he and others in his generation had enjoyed. His talents were immense, but his highest aspiration was to serve others.

John's ambitions were for social justice and democratic renewal, and throughout his life he harboured great hopes for what could be achieved through political action. Perhaps he put that life's mission best when he summarised the task of politics in the John Mackintosh Memorial Lecture:

> I believe . . . in democratic optimism, in our capacity as a nation to set our own objectives for the society in which we live, and to set about achieving them in a spirit of resolute determination. Neither our democracy, nor our aspirations for all its citizens need be thwarted by the power of the forces ranged against us nor by the implausible arguments to which they resort.
>
> We are, in the Labour Movement, guided by the high and ennobling principles of democratic socialism. Each generation must find its own way in the circumstances of its own time to give them practical effect. I believe that the challenge to us is to create the society which is productive and prosperous, but which shares its wealth with a sense of justice in the knowledge that it is not only a better way, but a more secure foundation. It is a challenge which can be met with confidence and with optimism.[33]

I am grateful to Delyth Evans for all her excellent work in bringing together John's speeches; to Douglas Alexander for research on John's early life and his views on devolution; to Colin Currie for help with drafting; and to Elizabeth Smith for showing me letters, articles and hitherto unpublished writings of John's. I am grateful also to Neil MacCormick and Bob McLaughlin for allowing the publishers to quote from their reminiscences of John's early life.

NOTES

1. 'Prosperity and Justice – the challenge of modern Socialism': John Mackintosh Memorial Lecture, Edinburgh University, 1 May 1987.
2. 'Reclaiming the Ground': The RH Tawney Memorial Lecture, 20 March 1993.
3. Ibid.
4. Ibid.
5. Ibid.
6. *Hansard*, 10 November 1970, Column 245.
7. *Hansard*, 15 May 1985, Column 328.
8. *Hansard*, 22 February 1984, Column 836.
9. *Hansard*, 15 March 1984, Column 528.
10. *Hansard*, 15 March 1984, Column 530–531.
11. 'A New Way Forward': Local Government Conference, Bournemouth, 7 February 1993.
12. *Hansard*, 15 March 1984, Column 534.
13. *Hansard*, 16 March 1988, Column 1116.
14. *Hansard*, 16 March 1988, Column 1117.
15. *Hansard*, 16 March 1988, Column 1126.
16. *Hansard*, 9 February 1989, Column 1155.
17. *Hansard*, 9 February 1989, Column 1159.
18. *Hansard*, 9 February 1989, Column 1166.
19. *Hansard*, 7 June 1989, Column 249.
20. *Hansard*, 24 October 1989, Column 689.
21. *Hansard*, 24 July 1991, Column 1193.
22. *Hansard*, 24 September 1992, Column 15–16.
23. *Hansard*, 24 September 1992, Column 15–17.
24. *Hansard*, 16 March 1993, Column 197–198.
25. *Hansard*, 9 June 1993, Column 288.
26. *Hansard*, 22 July 1993, Column 532.
27. Labour Europe Conference, Brighton, 6 November 1992.
28. 'The Public Service Ethos': RIPA, 8 May 1991.
29. 'The Standards and Practice of Government', London, 28 January 1993.
30. 'A Citizens' Democracy', London, 1 March 1993.
31. Local Government and Europe Conference, Glasgow, 6 February 1994.
32. COSLA Conference, Elgin, 1 April 1977.
33. 'Prosperity and Justice – the challenge of modern Socialism': John Mackintosh Memorial Lecture, Edinburgh University, 1 May 1987.

Tribute

by

Lord Irvine of Lairg QC

At Cluny Church, Edinburgh, on 19 May, Lord Irvine of Lairg QC paid tribute to his late friend.

John Smith's death evoked an outpouring of national grief without precedent in recent times. It crossed the political spectrum. It touched the whole country. Why? Because the public was ahead of the political analysts in its perception of John Smith. He had succeeded in communicating with the country and the signals back were affirmative.

John and I go back to 1959. He was then what he remained: a Highlander and so, to a degree, a romantic; a Presbyterian, not a Puritan, reared in the Church of Scotland; and a Labour Party family man. He was driven by a set of moral imperatives which owed everything to his inherited conscience. He gave equal value to every human being. He was a natural leader born with a compelling sense of public duty to improve the lives of every member of the community, especially the disadvantaged, by levelling up, not down.

He won the respect of the country by saying what he meant and meaning what he said. He was completely without side. He was as free of conceit or snobbery as it is possible to be.

He understood 'la condition humaine'. He was fascinated by quirks of language or behaviour of people high or low. He relished the absurd and his infectious merriment filled a room. I will never forget him whacking his knee with gusto in the telling of outrageous tales.

The media gave him the image of a staid Scottish bank manager or cautious Edinburgh lawyer. Prudent he certainly was, with the soundest judgment. But no one who has seen John on occasion in the role of Master of the Revels, leading from the front, can quite come to terms with the image.

Many have said that he brought his forensic skills to the cut and thrust of House of Commons debate. Too much is claimed for his profession. He respected it and was a fine practitioner. But he studied history for four years at his university before he ever opened a law book and by then his unique debating style and skills had been fully developed in the debating chamber of the University Union.

I remember encouraging him in 1974 in his decision to refuse the offer of the Solicitor Generalship of Scotland. Not for him a routine legal career in Parliament. The law was too small to accommodate him.

He was deadly in debate. No one could think faster on his feet. Under fire he never failed in counter attack. His opponents were a necessary part of a class act. But even in the exercise of his greatest skill there could be restraint.

In the Westland Debate in 1986 he was devastating, but abstained from cruelty when the opportunity was there.

John was a patriot, but he had the traditional ease of the Scots with Europe, untouched by nationalism. His one rebellion against his party was in 1971 when he was among the 69 Labour MPs to vote for Britain joining the European Community. His pro-Europeanism was consistent throughout his life.

John moved his party and his Church and above all his remarkable family. When he died, Elizabeth was by his side. The end was mercifully swift. Throughout his life he gave his friends fierce loyalty and we gave ours in return. We shall cherish his memory until our times are come.

Memorial Service for the Rt Hon John Smith QC MP

Address by

The Archbishop of Canterbury

A few chapters before the passage read today from Isaiah occur these matchless words: 'Have no fear, I have paid your ransom. I have called you by name and you are mine. When you pass through deep waters I am with you.'

John Smith is the name of everyman. That is fitting, because everyman is what John Smith the political leader stood for and worked for. It is a name loved and known by God: 'I have called you by name and you are mine.'

And today we celebrate the life and achievements of a man who delighted in ordinary people. His calling was to serve them and raise them high. His achievements and abilities were remarkable, yet he remained a humble person. For he saw the meaning of life in a God who took ordinary human form, who humbled himself, gave himself in service and love, and died for us all. That is the God who called John Smith by name, and in whom he now rests.

So across party lines, we now gather to remember with deep thanksgiving the Leader of Her Majesty's Opposition, John Smith QC, MP. There was nothing out of the ordinary about his Scottish upbringing. His father was the village schoolmaster. His family were Presbyterian in that undemonstrative way that is so refreshing about Scottish spirituality – devout and deep, but down to earth. The values of that home were simple. Honesty. Neighbourly care. Hard work. Fairness. Faithfulness. Service to others. They were not necessarily talked about much, they were the assumed way to behave.

It was natural for a bright young person to acquire from this background a sense of mission and to express it through participation in public life. By the age of 22 he knew he wanted to be a politician and which political ideals commanded his allegiance. His commitment to the Labour Party never wavered.

On the way to the fulfilment of his life's ambition he met a fellow student, Elizabeth, who was to become his dear wife. She too shared his goals and shared his life. Today it is right to acknowledge Elizabeth's huge contribution to his work and his deep love for her and their daughters.

John Smith loved people – ordinary people. He wanted all of them to have opportunities to develop their full potential. Social justice was his cause, rooted in his fierce and instinctive commitment to the worth of every living person made in the image of God. When I first talked to him at length, I was struck by the vividness and strength of his feelings, which he disciplined and channelled so effectively in public. He minded passionately about the life chances and dignity of ordinary people.

But he was consistent in his respect for other people, including his opponents. There were times, of course, when he felt alienated from others because of differences of ideology, or politics, but he regarded it as a weakness to attack a personality instead of the policies the person supported.

We find a typical expression of this respect for others in his essay *Reclaiming the Ground*. 'An ethical approach to life and politics,' he wrote, 'can be held as firmly by people of other faiths and by those who hold no religious convictions' as by Christians like himself. 'Nor,' he continued, 'should Christian socialists ever seek to suggest that Christians must be socialists. Because we, like Tawney, see our Christian faith as leading towards democratic socialist convictions, we must always recognise that fellow Christians might properly arrive at different conclusions from ourselves.'

Politics, as practised by John Smith and many others in all parties, is not a shallow or cynical pursuit. It is a way of serving the community, demanding hard work and high standards. As he himself wrote: 'Politics ought to be a moral activity and we should never feel inhibited in stressing the moral basis of our approach. Of course, we have . . . to undertake the intellectual task of applying a moral principle in a way which results in a practical policy of benefit to our fellow citizens . . . But let us never be fearful of saying that we espouse a policy because it is, quite simply, the right thing to do.'

He once startled his Radio One audience, and perhaps his advisers, by suddenly saying on air: 'You are not put on this earth to enjoy yourself!' But the truth is also that John Smith loved his work. He combined a strong sense of duty with a strong sense of humour and fun. His commitment was *strengthened* by his relish for people and life, not in conflict with it.

Many people have spoken of his integrity. Everybody could trust him, which is why he was a leader who healed divisions. Everybody knew that he was not in it for himself but was dedicated to serving other people as effectively as he could, as a Member of Parliament and as a national politician. As we remember his unostentatious moral integrity, we may recall the words of Vaclav Havel: 'I am deeply convinced that politics is not essentially a disreputable business and to the extent that it is so, it is only disreputable people who make it so.' John Smith was the very last person to claim he was anything other than a fallible human being like the rest of us. But the fact is that he showed that politics, despite all its compromises and temptations, can be a form of service to one's fellow human beings; a way of being faithful to one's beliefs about what is right and good.

For John Smith, this commitment sprang from the faith he was proud to own. During tributes in Parliament, it was delightfully said that he had 'all the virtues of Presbyterianism and none of its failings'. He was not one of those who confused being good with being miserable, and he was not too preoccupied with the sinful and wicked side of human nature. On the contrary, since God showed himself fully to us in Jesus Christ, 'bearing the human likeness, revealed in human shape', John Smith saw the reflection of the divine in ordinary people and everyday life. He had no time at all for the kind of religion which despises or turns its back on this world and its needs. He wanted God's will done on earth as it is in heaven.

Here was a brother Christian seeking, like many of us here from all parties and none, to live a Christian existence amongst all the contradictions and confusions of this complicated life. He never wore his faith on his sleeve. It breathed naturally through his life. He worked out his faith through what he was and what he did, bearing in mind the commitment to live and serve one another and value one another highly which is at the heart of the Christian revelation.

Christianity formed the centre of his life, a practical faith, a faith which for him was the justification for all the burdens and pains which a professional political life can bring. He followed the pattern urged by St Paul on the Philippians: 'Let your bearing towards one another arise out of your life in Christ Jesus.'

It is somehow right that John Smith's body lies in the graveyard of Kings on the beautiful island of Iona, home of the holy St Columba in the sixth century. John Smith went there last summer and I know from the Warden of the Community that each day he joined the Community for prayer in the sacred Abbey Church. Iona was the seedbed of Celtic Christianity, so formative in the history of Scotland and northern England. It is a place where the spiritual and earthly touch each other, and a fitting resting place for a Christian man whose integrity of life and commitment to the entire people of these islands is undisputed. A man who served God through politics.

Our hearts go out to Elizabeth, Sarah, Jane and Catherine who must now live without a man so dear and precious to them. Their joy and ours is to thank God for a life which will encourage us all, regardless of party or profession, a man who lives on in the hearts and hopes of so many people.

On behalf of John Smith's loved ones, his colleagues, friends and the people of this country about whom he cared so passionately, I offer as a final prayer to God these words written by St Columba of Iona himself. Let us carry them with us on our pilgrimages as John Smith did.

My dearest Lord,
be thou a bright flame before me,
be thou a guiding star above me,
be thou a smooth path beneath me,
be thou a kindly shepherd behind me,
today and for evermore.

Amen.

Part Two

*John Smith:
The Man*

Our Father

by

Sarah Smith

We decided as a family to become involved in the making of this book partly, as my mother has explained, to thank the many people who wrote beautiful letters to us, and partly because we as a family could provide unique insights into Dad's less public life. From our memories, and from a wide range of articles, speeches and interviews, we can go some way to explaining not just his political motivations but also his love of Scotland, the profound influence of his Argyll upbringing and what it was that motivated him to go into politics at all.

We include also a selection of the tributes that were published and the letters we received, because they made it clear to us that we were not alone in our grief. The letters in particular conveyed a sense of bereavement shared by very many people. It was a huge comfort to us to know that our father had been so widely loved.

Before 1993 I had never attended a Labour Party Conference. We were there as a family to provide support for Dad in the week when the hard-fought OMOV vote would be decided. It was our idea, not his. We hoped it would help him to relax at a very difficult time.

When on the Wednesday – after much tension and uncertainty – the vote was won, Dad was ecstatic. That night with family and colleagues he celebrated. And for Dad celebration, like everything else he did, was not something he did by halves. Though fond of telling us we had not been put on this earth to enjoy ourselves, he could rise to occasions like that. It was a wonderful celebration.

There were a lot of us, and lots of bottles of champagne. He felt the biggest test of his leadership so far was over, and there were sufficient grounds for a mighty party. At the end of a long night a deal was struck: the next really big celebration would be on the night of the general election. He was in no doubt about the outcome, and his preparations for victory included a large social dimension. He was always mindful of the fact that he hadn't been able to spend as much time with his family as he would have liked. He promised that our reward for sacrifices made for the sake of his career would come with a Labour Government. Chequers and Number 10 were going to be fun, starting with an even better party than the one just ending.

He gave us a marvellous grounding in life. As a wee boy from Ardrishaig, he had made it against the odds, first to a career at the Scottish Bar then to be Leader of the Opposition. To us he pointed out what advantages we had, and how inexcusable it would be to waste them or even take them for granted. He made it clear to us that every task had to be approached with honesty and integrity, and that whatever we did in life had to reflect both a useful purpose and a concern for others.

As someone who gave one hundred per cent to everything, he expected much from those around him. In political debate around the kitchen table he treated us as equals, with no concessions to be made on grounds of youth. We were allowed great independence of thought and action, the assumption being that we would be smart enough to learn from our own mistakes.

We were encouraged to follow our own paths. He did not steer any of us towards the law or politics. What he did expect was total commitment to the task in hand. He wouldn't tolerate poor exam performance when the problem was lack of effort or dedication – something he simply couldn't understand.

He was delighted when my youngest sister, Catherine, followed his footsteps to study law in Glasgow – entirely of her own accord. When Jane, my other sister, excelled in her studies at the Scottish College of Textiles, he was proud of her too. But he was less convinced of my own dedication: at my graduation from Glasgow University he insisted on pulling me into a lecture theatre just to make sure I'd seen the inside of one before I left for good.

In recent years he found family excuses for celebration, such as all five of us being together – a rarer and rarer event – in Edinburgh or London. It usually meant a big meal out, a lot to drink and a great deal of fun, Dad being a forceful and amusing character who made such evenings both hilarious and memorable.

He liked to enjoy himself and provide enjoyment for others too. Once, quite recently, he was stuck in London because of a TV commitment. As I was in London as well I phoned and suggested going to a film. A few hours later he had bought and prepared some marvellous food, sorted out tickets for the chosen film and generally made an evening of it. We saw *The Remains of the Day* and afterwards he put me in a taxi. I was terribly proud when the driver turned round as we left: 'That was the next British Prime Minister then?'

Perhaps my father's most important legacy to us as a family comes from his love of the Highlands and the Western Isles. He resisted our pleas for holidays in France or Spain, and I am glad now that he did. Our family holidays were in the West Highlands and we too came to be enchanted by their beauty and peace. Some of his writings about his beloved Highlands are to be found in this section of the book. His favourite island was Iona, where he rests now.

Edinburgh
August 1994

On Being a Father

After John's death the following short piece was found amongst his papers.

I have been involved in many responsibilities, ranging from that of a trial lawyer to a Cabinet Minister, but the most important and most fulfilling responsibility I have ever discharged is that of being a father.

I have three daughers now growing from teenagers into adulthood, and it is a big job to make sure that they realise their full potential. Above all, a father has to bear in mind that he sets an example which his children follow. To that extent, he can often make or mar their lives. That is quite a chilling as well as vital responsibility.

Thank God, it can also be very fulfilling and great fun.

My Scotland

John Smith was a Scot – and proud of it. In My Scotland *he explained why.*

My Scotland is a tangled intermixture of the Highlands and the Lowlands. I was nearly born in Islay where my father was then schoolmaster in the remote western village of Portnahaven. Perhaps for reasons of caution, my mother moved to have me in the village of Dalmally where, I suppose, medical facilities might be marginally more available. So I missed being a Hebridean although I imagine I must have made the trip by McBrayne's steamer up West Loch Tarbert *in embryo* en route to being born in Lorne. A few years later, the family moved to Ardrishaig in mid-Argyll where my father was for many years headteacher of the local primary school. It was, in many ways, an idyllic country childhood. In my early years, even the war hardly seemed to touch us. There must have been the privation of rationing, but they were doubtless softened by the locally caught fish and the eggs from the hens at the bottom of our expansive schoolhouse garden. I remember vaguely the glow in the sky over the hills to the east, which was said to be the effect of the fires burning in blitzed Clydebank, and the glamour of a visit on leave by my Uncle Peter, a Flying Officer in the Royal Air Force, resplendent in light blue uniform and pilot's wings. Not very long after he was shot down and killed over Holland on a pathfinder mission – so soon was the apparent glamour dissipated by the horrors of a war which did touch everyone almost everywhere.

Life in Ardrishaig revolved to a large extent around the Crinan Canal which starts its nine-mile journey to the western seas at the sea loch and basin where the main road cuts across the canal. I learned to love the sea and to this day I am never totally content if I am too far away from it. There was a steady – and stately – procession through the canal of puffers

119

(then in their heyday), yachts and other pleasure boats, and the sturdy fishing boats from Tarbert and the Ayrshire fishing ports en route to and from fishing grounds in the North. Some years later, when a law student at Glasgow University and stuck for a vacation job, I approached J & J Hamilton Ltd, then owners of a small fleet of puffers, for summer employment. An extremely sceptical manager in their Glasgow office had all his doubts dispelled when I explained that I came from Ardrishaig. That was proof positive that I knew about puffers. During that summer, I was deckhand, cook, second engineer, and 'the boy' on *The Invercloy*, a rather classy oil-fired puffer which went on longer voyages to the islands as well as dodging about on the Firth of Clyde. It was my best-ever vacation job. I learned to cook, even if peeling potatoes in one bucket while being sick in another while crossing the Minch on a stormy day is an unusual introduction to the culinary arts. My best memory is conversing with the skipper, a knowledgeable man from Appin, in the wheelhouse as we kept each other company on a night watch as the boat steadily pushed forward through the moonlit seas of the Inner Hebrides. We went to Barra to carry bricks and building materials for the rebuilding of Kismuil Castle, to Ulva, to Stein in Skye, to Diabaig in Loch Torridon, to the Islay distilleries, to Tobermory, the neat and tidy capital of the magnificent Island of Mull. We tied up at substantial piers but also beached the boat (puffers were flat-bottomed) on lonely Highland beaches where the locals came in carts and tractors to collect their annual delivery of coal.

It was a unique – and quite magnificent – introduction to the Western Isles and the start of a life-long attachment to them. For year after year, when the children were at an age when sand was more attractive than discos, we holidayed in Iona – to my mind, the almost perfect miniature of the Inner Hebrides. There is – as all *aficionados* will testify – something special about Iona. From this tiny island, the Columban missionaries reached as far as Northern Germany: on its sandy shores were brutal massacres of the pious monks by brutal marauding Vikings. Heaven, for me, is walking on the springy machair at the edge of a white Hebridean beach watching the summer sun sparkle on the ultramarine sea.

I first came in contact with more Lowland influences when at the age of 14, and after having attended Ardrishaig Primary School and Lochgilphead Junior Secondary, I moved on to Dunoon Grammar School for my senior secondary education. In those days – although happily not now – there was no senior secondary school in mid-Argyll and those wishing to proceed with an education beyond the age of 15 had to go to Dunoon or to Oban High School. I must have been in a less Highland mood than later as I opted for Dunoon, where I stayed in lodgings to attend the Grammar School for three years. I suppose it was an early lesson in independence, in fending for yourself. For some it worked, but sadly for many others it was a deterrent to further education. I am sure mid-Argyll is much better with its own school at Lochgilphead.

I enjoyed my years at the Grammar School, an institution which has been providing education for Cowal since the 15th century, and a useful reminder that many state schools in Scotland have a prouder history than some more pretentious establishments in the so-called private sector. Three of the 50 Scottish Labour MPs were educated at Dunoon Grammar – a record which might not attract universal approbation, but seems pretty good to me.

My next phase was at the University of Glasgow where I took like a duck to water to the political debating for which the student community is noted. It was a lively and vigorous time. I went to University in 1956 – the year of Suez and Hungary, the subjects of the first intense and passionate debates I attended. I managed to spend seven active years in University, from doing a History degree and the remaining three in law. It was a wise Scottish practice – now unfortunately discontinued – for lawyers to have a general education before tackling the laws of contract or conveyancing. My interest in politics was, not surprisingly, fostered in the Glasgow atmosphere and while still a law student I stood, at the age of 23, in the 1961 parliamentary by-election in East Fife as the Labour candidate. I did not do too badly, fighting off one of the perennial Liberal revivals to keep Labour second in a very traditional Tory seat by 90 votes. I was greatly helped by a flood of canvassers from my alma mater who descended on the unsuspecting constituency at weekends. I can now confess that they were not all members of the Labour Club: many forswore their normal allegiances for a weekend away supporting 'Glasgow's man'. I stood again in the general election of 1964, and in the intervening period I came to know that lovely part of Fife very well indeed. I was able to repay my debt to Fife years later when I helped the campaign in Parliament to preserve Fife intact as one of the new regions in the local government re-organisation of 1973.

Eventually, after a short period as a solicitor in Glasgow, I went to Edinburgh to join the Scottish Bar. Then – as in most cases now – you have to live in Edinburgh to practise effectively at the Bar. My wife and I got married in the year I was called and both of us had the reservations about moving to the East which people from the West of Scotland nearly all have, but which no one in Edinburgh understands. In no time we learned to love Edinburgh, one of Europe's great cities, where we have happily raised our family. I take equal pleasure in Glasgow's rise to prominence. Central Scotland is a tale of two cities, both different and genuinely complementary.

In 1970, I entered the Commons as Member for the famous constituency of North Lanarkshire. I was the first male Labour MP for many years, my predecessors being the much loved Peggy Herbison, and many years before her, Jennie Lee. There had been a Tory MP in between them because of a fractricidal split between the ILP and the Labour Party. That was my introduction to Lanarkshire – to the working people of the towns and villages I have had such pleasure and satisfaction in representing for the last 18 years. In 1983, North Lanarkshire – the sprawling northern landward part of the old county stretching from Bishopbriggs to Harthill – was abolished and I was happily adopted as their candidate by the new Monklands East constituency which comprises the whole of Airdrie, part of Coatbridge and the industrial villages surrounding Airdrie.

I like the plain no-nonsense matter-of-factness of my Lowland constituents, their warm and outgoing natures, their wealth of industrial skills, and the mixture of cultures which the swift changes of the industrial revolution brought together.

I have had – and have – a happy life in Scotland. I started as a Highlander and I suppose I am now much more a Lowlander. I suspect, however, that these old distinctions are now becoming much less meaningful. I am Scots – proud of it, and very glad to be able to live in and enjoy my own country – all of it.

I Love Islands

John Smith often recounted how he was 'nearly born on the island of Islay'. In this article he extolled the island way of life.

I love islands. Particularly for holidays. There is a special feeling about arriving on an island and seeing the boat depart. Apart from some unusual emergency circumstance you are irrevocably part of the island, part of its community, bound into its very nature by its isolation. Of course today you can be helicoptered to hospital if sudden illness or accident happens and the perils of being cut off are so much less than once they were. Despite all that there is something uniquely different – just a touch of excitement, however fanciful – about realising that you are now on an island which is not part of an indissoluble whole, that, even if only for short periods of time, you are cut off, that you are in a different – and in my opinion better – environment. This feeling is of special importance if the purpose of the vacation is to retreat from the relentlessness of a world which finds no time in its busy schedules for a pause for reflection and discounts the deep human need for periods of calm and peace.

I was nearly born on the island of Islay. My father was the dominie – the village schoolmaster – in the remote village of Portnahaven on the west coast of the island and my parents lived there in the schoolhouse – as I did for the first two years of my life. But in 1938 my parents apparently thought it prudent to move to the mainland for my arrival into the world and I was born instead in my grandmother's house in the village of Dalmally in Argyll. So I regard myself as almost a Hebridean. Naturally the islands which are special to me are the Inner Hebrides, the islands off the west coast of Argyll. Over the years since I have had so much pleasure from visits and holidays to these islands that they now have a special place in my life, almost in what I might pompously call my philosophy of existence.

The most beautiful island in the Inner Hebrides – perhaps in the world – is Mull. It has high hills – the largest is Ben More (the 'great hill' in Gaelic) – and from the Atlantic west long sea lochs drive into the interior. This combination provides landscapes of quite breathtaking beauty. If only Mull did not attract the rain (one minus factor of high hills) or provide the world headquarters for midges, it would truly be a heaven on earth. There are fortunately precautions against midges and it does not always rain. Sometimes when the sun is shining through after a rain storm has passed the island looks at its most magical.

The most mysterious island is Jura. Large in extent, dominated by the high rising Paps of Jura, separated from Scarba to the north by the whirlpool of Corryvrechan, it is almost entirely unpopulated. Glen and moorland are largely given over to the native deer. Despite its wilderness quality it is relatively easily accessible (as are most of the Inner Hebrides). This is no doubt why it proved attractive to writers like George Orwell who spent a time living and working in a lonely part of this lovely island.

Islay is a busy island. It is the home of efficient farms, of neat villages, like Bowmore, Port Ellen and Port Charlotte, and, of course, it is the home of one of the most important branches of the Scotch whisky industry. Here are made the peaty Islay malts with a distinctive flavour and character which makes them either leading single malts or essential elements in the blending process of other whiskies. Just as Jura is lonely and mysterious, Islay in contrast has a sense of bustle and order.

Of the other larger islands, Tiree and Coll are further out in the Atlantic and because they are low lying (Tiree particularly so), they have a remarkably high sunshine record. The rain clouds coming across the Atlantic pass well over them before they contact the hills of Mull and the mainland West Highlands. Like Colonsay to the south, these islands have long white beaches – a notable Hebridean characteristic. The beaches are white because they are made up of myriads of seashells and the contrast with the water creates an unforgettable ultramarine hue. The idyllic Hebridean circumstance is to walk along the crunchy white beach bordered by the blue green sea on a sparkling summer morning and then move inwards to walk over the springy turf (the 'machair') which stretches inland from the beach and is often covered in a carpet of wild flowers.

My favourite island – and the location of many happy family holidays – is the sacred isle of Iona where in AD 653 St Columba landed from Ireland to bring Christianity to Scotland – and much further afield. Small in extent and a mile or so off the south-west tip of Mull, it is almost the perfect miniature of a Hebridean island. But much more than that – it is a special place. That St Columba knew – as do his spiritual successors, the Iona Community, who have restored the Abbey over the last 50 years and who use the island as their principal base. When Dr Johnson visited Iona on his Hebridean tour he observed – as is recorded in a plaque on the road between the pier and the Abbey – 'That man is little to be envied, whose patriotism would not gain force upon the plains of Marathon or whose piety would not grow warmer among the ruins of Iona.'

Succeeding generations have also discovered the special quality of peace and piety of Iona. Literally thousands of visitors arrive in Iona on summer day trips across Mull from Oban and in the middle of the day they proceed from the pier to the Abbey and some even climb the small hill which is the island's highest vantage point. I think they all gain something – even if it is only a passing sense that there is something unique and different about Iona. Perhaps surprisingly, Iona's magic is not disturbed or in any way diminished by the crowds and after the last have departed across the Sound of Iona to Mull, by late afternoon it reverts almost imperceptibly to a quiet Hebridean haven.

These then are special islands. Beautiful in the subtle blends of colours and landscapes, exciting in the speedy changes of weather which pass over them, almost primeval in the enduring sense of timelessness. For me – and for many, many others – they are unique sources of refreshment and renewal.

The Munros

by

Murray Elder

When I first met John, he would describe one of his hobbies as hill walking. The evidence for this was however somewhat limited. There was an annual event, often rather elaborate, with as many as a couple of dozen walkers, followed by a splendid, and invariably convivial evening to follow.

Only after his heart attack in 1988 did he turn seriously to the hills, and walking was to become one of the great pleasures of his life.

He was happy to walk in the hills on his own, or with friends. Although there to get away from the political life, he immensely enjoyed stopping to chat to the many people who, recognising him, wanted to do so.

He was never bothered by the weather, but the sense of exhilaration when the day cleared, and the summits had been reached, was unmistakable – never more so than on Challum, as recorded here. He was born in Argyll, and, for all his love of the rest, he got especial pleasure on the hills that enabled him to look out on his native county – for that reason alone, Ben Cruachan was probably his favourite single day on the hills, and has left me with one of my happiest memories.

Since John died, a number of people, some of whom simply met him on the hills, have suggested that there should be some appropriate memorial to John as a hill walker. That will need to be done with care, as John cared deeply about the preservation of the wildness of the Scottish hills. For the time being, it is nice to see in print a few pages of his own memories of his days in the Scottish hills.

The Munros

The following is the edited text of a foreword for a book on his beloved Munros which John Smith provided for his constituent and friend, Peter Drummond.

I climbed Ben Challum. It was a cold winter's day and as we gathered at Kirkton Farm the frost was hard on the ground and the cloud hung over the hill. As I laced up my boots I thought to myself that while I was determined to get to the top, this might be one of the many similar outings on which I saw very little from the summit. How wrong I was. About 1000 feet up we broke through the cloud inversion and entered a magical world. The sky was blue, the sunlight reflected on the snow, and above an all-encompassing sea of cloud all we could see in every direction was mountains.

To the south the Crianlarich Hills and the Arrochar Alps, to the east the Lawers group, to the west Cruachan, and to the north and north-west Ben Nevis itself and the Mamore hills. I do not believe there was a better place to be on the face of the earth that winter's day than on the top of a Scottish mountain.

Although I was born in the shadow of Cruachan, I only came to mountaineering late in life. But I cannot adequately express the enjoyment I have had from the experience. Climbing the hills as a conscious recreation is only a hundred years old but I am glad to say it is becoming ever more popular. All of us who enjoy the Scottish mountains owe a debt of gratitude to the redoubtable Sir Hugh who tabulated the Munros. But we also ought to pay our grateful respects to the first man to climb them all, the Reverend A. E. Robertson. Had he not pioneered the ascent of all the Munros – I hesitate to attach the slightly pejorative description of 'The first Munro-bagger' to a Victorian divine – would others have followed in his path? Would Scottish mountaineering have become the popular and fast-growing sport that it has undoubtedly become today?

A Change in Lifestyle

John Smith's heart attack in 1988 encouraged a change in lifestyle and attitude. In this article for the Guardian *he reflected on the changes.*

Near to my home in Edinburgh is the Hermitage of Braid. It is a delightful park – once a local landowner's small estate – which was generously gifted to the city by Mr John McDougal, a local citizen, just before the Second World War. I have had frequent cause to thank Mr McDougal – and the City Council who now have care of the lands – during my several months of convalescence from a heart attack. I was told to diet and to exercise, one a penance, the other a pleasure. Of the dieting, more later.

I have always enjoyed walking – usually in the wilder stretches of my native Highlands where the sweep and grandeur of the high hills are an irresistible lure. But I have learned a different and highly congenial form of exercise among the tall trees and the leaf-covered walks in the valley in the Hermitage of Braid. I have learned that walking is not just a long slog upwards as an almost Calvinistic condition precedent to the enjoyment of a traverse over the tops and the glories of the vista from the heights. On my daily perambulations, I have learned to love walking of a quite different kind. If the mountains are grand opera, this was a Schubert song. It is principally – or so it seems to me – about observation. Observation of the fast-flowing burn, of the silhouetted framework of the leafless tree, of the hopping birds in the branches and hedgerows of winter, and of the clouds scudding across the changing sky. It is the feel of the leaves underfoot. There are so many in the Braid valley that they are burned in little piles – wisps of smoke rising upwards and glimpsed coming round a bend. But best of all is my friend, the heron.

I first saw him about lunchtime on a brisk day in November, standing impassive and motionless in the waters of the burn, just below

131

a weir near where the woods end. He was contemplating his lunch. I waited too, in the hope that I might see the flurry of the catch. Alas, it was not to be. Something disturbed him and he took off aloft – his wide wings bearing him away to other haunts – perhaps to the North Sea coast or the sanctuary at Duddingston Loch, both only a few miles away as the heron flies. Now, when I reach the spot, I always look for him. Some days I see him in my favourite setting – steadily watching the waters bubbling over the edge of the weir. On other days, he is further down the burn – perched on the far bank and still on watch. Some day I will have the joy of participating in the catch; it is a pleasure but postponed. In the meantime, there is the consolation of seeing the majestic flight of this most elegant of birds when, as at least sometimes happens, his patience runs out before that of his admiring observer.

Despite my genuine delight in this new-found pleasure of gentle walking, I have not given up the other. Just before Christmas, I took myself up Caerketton and Allermuir, the Pentlands tops, which overlook Edinburgh from the south, to see once again the low line of the Moorfoot Hills, the Castle, the Forth, the old volcano of Arthur's Seat, the trim cliffs of the Salisbury Crags and the further hills of Fife. I still like the opera, but I like to think I have learned some other happy – and I hope enduring – melodies.

Walking is fun, but dieting is not. For years, I have experimented with diets, all of which have ended in defeat and ignominious recrimination. But at last I had a motivation strong enough to overcome my shaming indiscipline. Strangely enough, it was not just the strong desire to get well again soon – powerful though that was, and is. What made me stick to it, through day after slimming day, was much more simple. I knew I had to go back to the Royal Infirmary to report – back to those doctors and nurses who had cared for me with such skill and concern, who had rescued me from the edge of death, who had given me the chance to try again. I could not – I would not – go back to them to confess failure. I could not – I would not – admit that despite all they had done for me, I could not do a little bit for myself.

I suppose it had a lot to do with pride, even more than self-preservation. I had learned enough – in the course of a Presbyterian upbringing – about the sins of pride, and no politician – whoever else – could be unaware of these pitfalls. There is on the other hand a positive side to pride, at least in the matter of slimming. Mind you, after a while the pride is replaced by a less attractive aura of self-satisfaction greatly encouraged by much welcomed observations from all and sundry on how much weight you have lost, how well you look, and how much better you must be for it all. The only corrective to the endless flow of self-congratulation is the sobering realisation that so many of them are taking the opportunity of reminding you of how awful you must have been before.

Despite that, I still have enough pride – and self-satisfaction – to feel confident about offering some words of advice to fellow aspirant slimmers. The first is that it ought not to be necessary to have a heart attack to find sufficient motivation. Some other stimulus must be found – some other commitment must be made from which it would be shaming to resile. In the House of Commons they – the parliamentarians, the hacks, and some others – join Spencer's Club (once named the Club for the Well Proportioned) for a publicised commitment to lose a stone over about six weeks, with a financial penalty for the losers. This all sounds splendid until it is appreciated that the penalties are used to pay for an expansive lunch at the end of the period, that many from the Whips' Offices take part, and that the much liked President of the Club is a distinguished Lobby Correspondent of the *Guardian* upon whose frame the ravages of fasting are not yet evident. I feel entitled to point out some of these deficiencies as a member of the Club myself – occasionally a success, in more recent years more often a failure. For some it works: for others, visibly not. The lesson must be – find some – any – motivation.

If that is not entirely helpful, let me offer some more soundly based advice on technique. Do not follow those who tell you all you need to do is to give up some fattening foods and indulge yourself on all the others. I found that the only way to diet was to count the calories just as the only way to lose weight is to eat less. In my mind, the two are inextricably linked. I set a level of 1,000 calories per day which is pretty severe, but achievable without excessive suffering. In most cases, 1,500 calories or more would do the trick, but for some people – like me – there needs to be evidence of dramatic progress to sustain the motivation and for such sinners, the lower figures are more effective. Of course, the calorific values have to be learned. That is not too difficult with the use of the excellent guides now available. The values of commonly used foods are easily remembered, and with a bit of practice, one can become adept at a quick calorific assessment. Perhaps most usefully of all, it makes you pause and consider before you eat.

I try to follow a pattern which goes like this. Breakfast is All Bran with milk (200 calories). Lunch is a consommé weight-reducing soup and one or two apples (again about 200 calories). Dinner is a weight-reducing frozen meal (a very good variety is available and is expanding fast) which is under 300 calories and which can be supplemented by a fairly substantial plate of vegetables (200 to 300 calories at most). If you go over the top on a day like Christmas Day, you cut down on the days after, or, if you are really disciplined, on the days before. If the week looks as if it is getting out of control, a day's starvation acts both as a penance and a smart means of reducing the average. I don't know if this would work for everyone – probably not. All I can give – as they say in evangelical circles – is my personal testimony. It worked for me. Down two stones and a bit. I am still at it to lose another. Two simple truths are that you have to eat less, and alcohol is not a friend. My one serious lapse – as my friends will not be surprised to hear – came from that quarter. But the encouraging moral of my story is surely this – if I can do it, who cannot?

It took a trauma to bring me to my senses, but in the course of what has been a surprisingly enjoyable convalescence, I have learned a new discipline, and some new pleasures. As well as walking, I have rediscovered reading – not the snatched absorption of the material of too many newspapers and periodicals in a great gobble of facts – but the joys of the novel, the biography, the history book.

I look forward to returning to the political fray, much fitter (I believe) and a shade more reflective (I hope). Many will say there was much room for such improvement. Above all, I go back as a very grateful person. Grateful beyond reckoning to a loving and supporting family and to the devoted carers of our National Health Service. I have but one political reflection. It cannot be bad for a putative Chancellor of the Exchequer to learn at first hand, and in dramatic circumstances, the crucial importance to us all of our vital public services. And to be given a little space and time to ponder upon it.

Immortal Memory

John Smith loved the songs and poems of Robert Burns primarily because they expressed 'a view of the world and of life which sees us all bound together in ties of mutual dependency, mutual enjoyment, mutual respect'.

Robert Burns is admired, respected and revered, not only through our sister European countries, but right across the world. He is not our exclusive property – he belongs to the world – but he is oor ain and since not every country chooses a poet as its national hero, we are, I think, entitled to a special pride in his immortal memory.

Born over 230 years ago, in a Scotland on the edge of the Industrial Revolution – and living through the excitements of the French Revolution and its aftermath – his life, short though it sadly was, was lived in a truly formative period, on the threshold of the modern world. He was the inheritor of a Scots literary tradition most recently exemplified by Allan Ramsay and Robert Fergusson. Unlike some earlier Scots poets, he chose, like Fergusson, to write in what he called the Scots dialect. The Kilmarnock edition in 1786 was described as 'Some poems chiefly in the Scots dialect'. It had been the habit to speak in Scots, but write in English tipped with Scots – or Scots tipped with English. That of course was the language all around – in his family and among the tenant farmers of Ayrshire. From the start, Burns wrote about life around him. Early in 1783, he began to keep a Commonplace Book in which he entered his poems and songs and his thoughts about life. And he began by writing about love. In April 1783, in the Commonplace Book he noted, 'I never had the least thought or inclination of turning Poet until I got once heartily in love and then rhyme and song were in a manner the spontaneous language of my heart.'

Even at this early stage, we can detect one of Burns' unique qualities – an identification with humanity, particularly through his own emotions

135

and that of the people around him. He spoke directly to and of the people which is why he still – centuries later – can touch their hearts. Characteristically he described his motivation light-heartedly:

> Some rhyme a neebor's name to lash,
> Some rhyme (vain thought) for needfu cash,
> Some rhyme to court the countra clash
> An raise a din
> For me an aim, I never fash,
> I rhyme for fun

He once, disarmingly, described his writing as 'stringing blethers up in rhyme'.

He may have rhymed for fun – and fun there is in plenty – in *Tam O' Shanter*, in the *Jolly Beggars* and in the *Merry Muses of Caledonia* there is the fun of human frailties and foibles sympathetically, if sometimes satirically, observed. There is also joy in the raptures of love and deep involvement in the tenderness of the most delicate human relations.

Although he was born among the ordinary people from whom his affection never strayed despite being lionised when adopted by the *literati* of Edinburgh, he was far from being an unlettered peasant – 'The Heaven-taught plowman' of legend. He was well taught, particularly in both the English and Scottish literary traditions. He drew from a strong intellectual background, but he chose to write in a direct and often homespun manner – using intellectual devices, using all the techniques of an accomplished poetic craftsman, acknowledging his debt to his intellectual progenitors, Ramsay and Fergusson (particularly Fergusson), and at the same time to a wider knowledge of English and classical literature, but he almost always wrote with exceptional directness and without affectation in a way which connected him directly with a large and ordinary public. When he strayed from this approach – under the influence of fashion or to please his patrons – his impact sharply diminished. But when he spoke, for example, about the Scottish countryside, he could do so in a direct and deeply engaging manner. Take the opening of *The Holy Fair*, a satire of a Mauchline Holy Fair – a festival of tent preaching which accompanied the open air communions held by the Calvinist church of his day. *The Holy Fair* appeared in the Kilmarnock edition although he judged it prudent to leave out *Holy Willie's Prayer* – a more biting satire on false and hypocritical piety. *The Holy Fair* was written in the old Scots tradition of poems describing popular festivities – it owed a deal to Fergusson's *Leith Races* which was written in the same burlesque manner. But it opens by spontaneous enjoyment of the countryside.

> Upon a simmer Sunday morn,
> When Nature's face is fair,
> I walked forth to view the corn,

An' snuffd the caller air.
The rising sun, owre Galston Muirs,
Wi glorious light was glintin;
The hares were hirplin down the furs,
The Lav'rocks they were chantin
Fu' sweet that day.

The poem goes on, in ironic humour, to describe rival preachers appealing to audiences, much under the influence of drink, contrasting the ostensible piety of the occasion with the profaning of much of the human activity. The concluding stanza combines the themes:

How monie hearts this day converts
O' sinners and o' lasses!
Their hearts o' stane, gin night, are gane
As saft as onie flesh is:
There's some are fou o' love divine;
There's some are fou o' brandy;
An' monie jobs that day begin,
May end in houghmagandie
Some ither day.

If we have any visitors here to whom *houghmagandie* is a novel description, let me just say it describes one of humanities most basic activities and the context should reveal its meaning in full.

The range of Burns' poetry was wide – as wide as the world around him. He adopted the Scots tradition of annual poems as in *The Twa Dugs*. He commented with sympathy as well as satire on the society he lived in the *Cotter's Saturday Night* – a sympathetic picture of a pious family which can be compared with the biting satire of the attack on the doctrine of predestination as well as hypocrisy in *Holy Willie's Prayer*.

On predestination:

O Thou that in the Heavens does well,
wha, as it pleases best Thysel,
sends ane to Heaven an' ten to Hell
A' for Thy Glory,
And no for onie guid or ill
They've done before Thee!

And on Willie's hypocrisy:

But, Lord, remember me and mine
Wi' mercies temporal and divine,
That I for grace an' gear may shine
Excell'd by nane;

137

And A' the glory shall be Thine –
Amen, Amen!

His contempt was not uniquely reserved for some of the religious ideas of his day. He always found the classification of society into landlords and tenants, into a gentry and a poor folk, hard to stomach.

In *The Twa Dugs*:

I've noticed, on our laird's court-day,
(An' monie a time my heart's been wae),
Poor tenant bodies, scant o' cash,
How they maun thole a factor's snash:
He'll stamp an' threaten, curse an' swear
He'll apprehend them, poind their gear;
While they maun staun' wi' aspect humble,
An' hear it a', an' fear an' tremble!

And his radicalism – his belief in the essential equality of all mankind – is most notable in the contempt of:

Ye see yon birkie ca'd 'a lord',
Wha struts, an' stares an' a' that?
Tho' hundreds worship at his word,
He's but a cuif for a' that.

By the Kilmarnock edition (although they were not all published then) Burns had completed the bulk of his poetic repertoire. With one notable exception his latter period was devoted to his song writing and collection, but in 1791 he published one of his master works, *Tam O' Shanter*. Based on an old folk tale about Alloway Kirk, it is a sustained verse narrative of verve, pace, humour and drama of a kind unique in Scottish and European literature. Although written mostly in Scots, and using the euphony of the Scots dialect –

She tauld thee well thou was a skellum,
A blethering, blustering, drunken blellum

– it is recited around the world. In *Tam O' Shanter* Burns showed himself – in the unique craftsmanship, the sense of drama, the joy in storytelling – as a dramatist, as well as a poet. Sadly it was the only example of such a poetic form in his works.

But the glory of Burns is in his songs. David Daiches – not only a noted Burns scholar, but a distinguished critic of English literature as a whole – described Burns as the greatest song-writer Britain has produced.

The last years of his life were devoted – for no rewards – to the collection, refashioning and preservation of the great folklore tradition in the songs of rural Scotland. But he did more than collect, edit, and preserve: he refurbished and rebuilt many of the stanzas and phrases: he created as well as collected. With enthusiasm for the lively and warm-hearted culture of his own people, he preserved and reshaped the whole body of Scottish folk song. Not only did he rescue the words – with a deft musical touch, he fitted the traditional airs to the fragments of song in a truly memorable achievement.

And what songs! Covering the range of human emotion – they express with a sharp directness and an often searing honesty the feelings of the ordinary people – their joys, their sorrows, their hopes, their sentimentalities. The sense of remembered friendships in *Auld Lang Syne* – a song which has literally encircled the world – an older song substantially rewritten for which Burns did not claim the inventive credit, but without his attention it would most probably have been forgotten. Many of the songs are love songs. Not just the expression of love, in tenderness or in rapture, but wistful and bitter sweet. We think of the lines he gives to his own Jean when she is about to bear his child:

> *O, wha my babie clouts will buy?*
> *O, wha will tent me when I cary?*
> *Wha will kiss me where I lie?*
> *The rantin dog, the daddie o't!*

Or consider the touching tenderness of the Burns' song of elderly love – with its roots in recollection and a life spent together:

> *John Anderson my jo, John,*
> *When we were first acquent,*
> *Your locks were like the raven,*
> *Your bonnie brow was brent;*
> *But now your brow is beld, John,*
> *Your locks are like the snaw,*
> *But blessings on your frosty pow,*
> *John Anderson my jo.*
>
> *John Anderson my jo, John,*
> *We climb the hill thegither,*
> *And monie a cantie day, John,*
> *We've had wi' ane anither;*
> *Now we maun totter down, John,*
> *And hand in hand we'll go,*
> *And sleep thegither at the foot,*
> *John Anderson my jo.*

139

Or that wonderful song, written after his parting from Clarinda –

> *Ae fond kiss, and then we sever,*
> *Ae farewell, and then forever!*

– with the haunting lines which Walter Scott said contained the essence of a thousand love tales –

> *Had we never lov'd sae kindly,*
> *Had we never lov'd sae blindly,*
> *Never met – or never parted –*
> *We had ne'er been broken-hearted.*

There are lively songs – *Corn Rigs Are Bonie:*

> *Corn rigs, an' barley rigs,*
> *An' corn rigs are bonie:*
> *I'll ne'er forget that happy night,*
> *Amang the rigs wi' Annie.*

There are the raucous and bawdy songs of the *Merry Muses of Caledonia*. Songs of patriotism, songs of pride – but all songs of Scotland and her people are still a living vibrant part of our folklore and culture. For that, we thank, as we should, Robert Burns.

But there is more to Burns than the literary monuments he left behind. There was – there is – Burns the man who appeals enduringly to people, particularly to the people of Scotland whose values and whose sense of patriotism he shared. Throughout his work run themes which are part of a long-standing Scots tradition: a tradition which I believe is strongly with us today. It can be expressed in many different ways, but it is a view of the world and of life which sees us all bound together in ties of mutual dependency, mutual enjoyment, mutual respect; which sees through the artifice of class distinction and privilege, built on such a flimsy pretext as money: which cuts through it all to see the ordinary man and the ordinary woman – with all their faults, but also with their manifest virtues – as the centrepiece of God's creation and gives them their rightful place 'abune them a'', which is based on the liberty of people and of nations and aspires for a world in which we'll 'brothers be for a' that'. It is a view of society which – whatever opinions there are in the rest of the kingdom – is shared by the majority of Scots who believe we live in one society and are locked together by the bounds of common humanity. And I believe Burns would have gloried in what has been called the importance of the democratic intellect, as one of the touchstones of Scottish life. He would have approved of the notion that the doors of opportunity must always be open to everyone. He lived very much in the Scotland of his day, but he spoke to generations in later centuries and across a wider world which is why his is truly an immortal memory.

Near the end of his life – in what I believe is one of his finest songs, he gave his thanks to Jessie Lawers, who nursed him in his last illness.

> *O wert though in the cauld blast*
> *On yonder lea, On yonder lea*
> *My plaidie to the angry airt,*
> *I'd shelter thee, I'd shelter thee*
> *Or did Misfortune's bitter storms*
> *Around thee blaw, around thee blaw*
> *Thy bield should be my bosom,*
> *To share it a', to share it a'.*

To share it a' is what we do with Robert Burns.

John Smith's Final Speech

John Smith's last speech – on the evening preceding his sudden death on 12 May 1994 – was at a European Gala Dinner in London. This edited version of the speech reflects many of his sustained beliefs.

Tonight we are engaged in a European Gala Dinner and it is interesting that we have had here tonight the Leader of the French Socialist Party, because we at the Labour Party are committed to the vision of the Europe that is most economically successful and socially just, which is why we are committed to the Social Charter. In the course of the campaign for the European elections, we will have the issues posed very clearly for the people of this country. On the one hand, we will have a Government which says the only way towards prosperity in Britain is to have the lowest wages, to have the poorest conditions and is hopeful that we will attract investment on that ground. But anyone who understands modern business and modern industry understands very clearly that that is the most foolish of views because there will always be people in the difficult world in which we live who will be able to undercut us on that assumption. Britain's future depends on investment in the skills of our able people, investment in our industry, particularly our manufacturing industry and in a partnership between Government, industry and business that makes sure that this country succeeds because of consistent investment in the very best training that any country can provide for its people. One of the ambitions of the next Labour Government is to create the best educated and trained workforce in the whole of Europe. In workforce, I include management. I believe 99 per cent of the people of this country would wish that as an objective. But what they have not had for 15 years is a Government that made that its objective. And if there is one single thing that the next Labour Government can do, it will be to make education and training the absolute star in the policies we propose so that at the end of our period of Government – I hope it will be ten years and perhaps it will be 15 years – but whatever it is, people will say at the end of it, 'this is the one country in the whole of Europe which does its very best for its young people'. Let everybody follow their abilities as far as they will take them and as far as their ambitions dictate. There can be no better ambition for a Government to wish for its people and I cannot think there are not intelligent industrialists, financiers, bankers, managers who don't share that vision for the future, which is why I welcome tonight so many representatives from the world of industry, finance and banking, probably more than we have ever had at a Labour Party Dinner in our history. It is right that they should be here because the Labour Party is the party that understands modern industry, modern society, modern finance and modern economics but also understands that the crucial raw material of our future is the skills of our people. There is a new duality to be created, as Gordon Brown, our Shadow Chancellor, constantly says. It is the connection between investment in technology and investment in people. And the investment in people has to be accompanied by the acknowledgement of the dignity of people. If we ask people to be responsible, we must give them rights as well. We must say to them, you are not to be exploited, which is why we are unequivocally in favour of a minimum wage, for the Social Charter, for decent conditions, because I don't think there should be an industrialist or financier who wants to employ people who are not employed under decent and reasonable conditions. Now, that is the message that we will be taking to our people in the European election. It is the message we have carried through all our campaigns and we will be taking it right through to the general election.

Now, we are going to go into the European elections, not arguing for referendums, not arguing for a sceptical view of Europe, not hesitant about our future in Europe. We are going to approach the European elections with a sense of vision and of purpose because we in the Labour Party believe that our future is truly in Europe, that the sum of the parts that we can create in the European Community is far greater than what we can achieve on our own and that the scale of events that the modern world requires, the intensive commitment it needs, the techniques it requires for effective government, require a proper European approach. That is why the Labour Party is now the European Party in British Politics. We are totally committed to it and we are going to sign up for the Social Charter which every other country in the European Community wants, and which significantly the four new countries, whom we are proud to welcome, in the Community, also want, because we have a balanced view of Europe. We want a successful Europe for business. We have a single market. Let's make a success of it.

But it is not enough for business to be successful. No business can be successful without reference to the people it employs or the community in which it survives. We must let prosperity spread throughout all our people and that is one of the visions that the European Community brings to the world and one which we are happy to subscribe to and support in what we do. We will fight the European elections on these policies and we will fight proudly because we are clear and confident about the European mission not only of our Party but of our country, and when we have a Labour Government, it won't be a Government which the rest of Europe just looks at slightly suspiciously and says, 'What are they up to now?' It will be a Government that proudly takes its place because it believes in the concept of Europe as much as all the other member states gathered round the table.

I think there is a great hunger amongst our people. There is a great hunger amongst our people for a return to politics of conviction and idealism. The Thatcher years proved that it was not possible for people to be successful and content simply by being successful on their own part because there were so many that had not been successful and the menace of high unemployment still threatens our society. The mission of the Labour Party must be to get Britain back to work, to get the people who are unemployed now employed in the useful work that needs to be done in building houses for people without homes, in building a new transport infrastructure for this country, and starting regional development on a scale that has never been attempted properly in this country, bringing not only power but economic success back to every region in this country, empowering industry and local authorities by a participating Government, a partnership Government that says that if you are prepared to commit yourself to the success of your country, your Government will be behind you. That applies at home and it applies abroad – a Government that supports British industry when it fights for orders abroad, supports the investment in technology and science which is desperately needed in our country. I think we are one of the most able countries on the face of the earth, certainly one of the most able countries in Europe, and the skills of our people – underdeployed by our Government.

But it must not be a Government which imagines that it can decide everything for business or decide everything for people. It is above all an enabling Government. A Government which seeks to share power, to enable power, to give them the chance to give of their best. I think that is the style of modern society and it ought to be the style of modern Government. I think that Government has to insist on certain important qualifications to business effort. It must say to all our businesses and all our people, you must respect the environment in which we live. You must respect the social rights of our people but you run your own business. You run them well and you run them successfully and we will be happy about that. But it will be in your interest to respect our environment and to respect our social rights and to give power to your people, and to clever and intelligent people working in your companies and in your industries. I think that is the message that Britain wants to

145

hear. But there is, perhaps, the most important message of all – no society, no country can ever survive to be successful without a profound sense of social justice and unless we bring social justice back to this country, this country cannot be healthy and cannot be successful.

When I go campaigning round this country and I meet the old age pensioners who are having to pay the VAT on fuel, I see the poor people who are struggling to make ends meet. One understands what social justice means when I meet the people who are dependent on state education for the future of their children, when I meet the vast majority of the people of this country who depend on the National Health Service for the health of their families, and they know – don't they know! – what is happening to our NHS. Ministers can produce statistic after statistic but our people who are connected to the Health Service from the moment they are born until the moment that many of them die, know the truth about our National Health Service and they know one wonderful truth about the Labour Party. If the Labour Party did nothing else in all its history, to have founded the National Health Service and lifted the care and worry from our people and founded a Health Service which was only to do with human need and not to do with money and access, or to do with privilege or anything else, they would know that the Labour Party had achieved a great virtue. But now we have to come back and restore it once again. So when you sum up all the issues we have in this country – social justice, economic justice, conquering unemployment, giving our young people the opportunities they ought to have in a modern Europe and a modern world, it adds up to a stunning case for Labour.

I am glad to say that our Party has been reinvigorated in recent years. This is now a confident Labour Party that you see meeting here tonight and can I say to those of our guests who may not be totally committed to our case, thank you for coming to us and thank you for listening to our case tonight? I think we have a strong, powerful and persuasive case. It is one which will be assisted by your contribution here tonight. It is one, I can tell you, which will be persisted in. Because this is a Labour Party that is determined to win. We believe in the idealism of our cause but we also believe it is not enough to be idle idealists who think we should just announce policies and hope that somehow people will come to them. We have to go out, argue fiercely, everywhere and in every town and hamlet and part of this country.

There is something fundamental happening in this country now. I suppose the academics would call it a circular shift in political attitudes. But we all know that it is happening. People who for years have been Conservatives have lost the faith and many people who sat on the edge of British politics have realised there is only one way forward for this country and that is to get installed in this country a Government with purpose, pragmatism and economic determination and also for social justice. I believe that everything is moving in our way. We must never be complacent and must never take anything for granted but I believe the signs are set fairer for the Labour Party than they have been for a very long time.

Thank you all very much for coming here tonight and helping us perhaps partly to achieve that objective. We will do our best to reward your faith in us but please give us the opportunity to serve our country. That is all we ask.

Desert Island Discs

On 28 May 1991, while John Smith was Shadow Chancellor of the Exchequer, he appeared as guest 'castaway' on the popular radio programme Desert Island Discs. *This relaxed discussion about his life seems a fitting way to end this part of the book.*

Sue Lawley My castaway this week is a politician. In many quarters he is now seen as the Opposition's strongest weapon in the forthcoming electoral battle with the Government. It might not have been so. Two and a half years ago he was struck down by a heart attack which could have ended his career but he returned to the political fray trimmer, fitter and, some say, even more incisive than before. His principles may be those of a good Scottish Socialist but his talents are those of a barrister. Supporters chuckle and opponents wriggle when he puts his inquisitorial skills into practice. He is the Shadow Chancellor of the Exchequer, John Smith. Simply that, John Smith? No more, no less?

John Smith No, I was called after my grandfather who was a fisherman in the village of Tarbert in Argyll and it was a family tradition to call the eldest boy after his father's father and the eldest girl after the mother's mother – it's not very original but I suppose it meant that the same names kept repeating through the generations.

SL But has it been an advantage or a bit of a disadvantage?

JS It's never worried me. I must say my parents had a bit of courage actually, not even putting a middle name of any kind in between and in the sort of confraternity of John Smiths I don't count the people with middle names, I don't think they are full strength somehow. But there's quite a lot of us about and of course if you open the telephone book you will see nothing but it and every time you, say, have to fill in a form, there is your name, Smith, John.

SL The distinguishing factor also though, of course, is you're Scottish.

How important is that to you?

JS Oh, it's very important, I think. It's important to all Scots. It certainly is important to me. I live in Scotland, I'm very much born and brought up there, I like it very much. I've got a deep loyalty to Scotland and I suppose I think the Scots are *the* people of the UK and I'm not saying this with prejudice to the others but I feel we have the most developed sense of this. I feel that these days anyway and I have been intricately involved with Scottish issues like Devolution and things like that over the years.

SL You say you live in Scotland but of course you live in London for most of the week and you left your family behind in Scotland, on purpose. Is it that you feel that the Scottish education and Scottish accent is, in a sense, for you anyway, superior?

JS No, it's not superior, but it gives a person an identity and I felt my children should be educated in Scotland which I must say I have confidence in it there, and, again, without prejudice to others, but I just believe it's better worked out and I think . . .

SL You mean you do think it's superior?

JS Aah, well, I think I'm forced to admit that, but then I think a lot of things could be copied from Scotland, as it happens. But, then, I'm biased.

SL What about the accent? Do you think it's superior?

JS I think it's clear, but of course it's not superior. But it's real and I felt that the children should know where they came from, especially in the world of politics. I think it's awfully sad when you see these sort of diplomatic children who have lived in every capital in the world but don't know where they come from. I wanted mine to feel that, at least, whatever they did afterwards, if they went to the ends of the earth, they knew where they sprang from, what they were all about.

SL What would happen if a Labour Government won the next election? Would you then be prepared to move south of the Border and move your wife, at least, into No 11 Downing Street.

JS I think I would and I would be free to do so because they have now left school and will have left school by then and I think probably with a job like Chancellor you've really got to be on the spot.

SL What about your Desert Island? Now is that a Scottish one? Where do you imagine it to be?

JS I thought it was in the South Seas somewhere. With palm trees and sand, quite a lot of sand. I didn't think it was up some lonely loch.

SL It's wherever you want it to be.

JS Well, I'll take it in the South Seas, I think.

SL And what sort of music will keep your misery at bay on it?

JS Well, quite a wide variety of music. My tastes are pretty wide but opera is quite an important interest and I've got increasingly interested in opera and orchestral music in recent years. I didn't arrive at it on my own. I followed my wife who is an opera fanatic and I sort of tailed along behind her to operas and then I got interested myself. I like

Scottish songs and I like odd things like Country and Western. I would take a mixture of things with me.

SL So what's the first one?

JS The first one is a Gaelic hymn, *Child in a Manger*, which is an old Gaelic tune called *Bunessan* from Bunessan in Mull. I think it was written by a lady called Mary MacDonald in the 19th century and it has become all sorts of other things. It's become the tune for *Morning Has Broken* but it's an old Gaelic tune to start with and I think it's a lovely tune.

SL The Gaelic version of *Child in a Manger*, from Bunessan in Mull and conducted by Rodney MacKenzie. A folk song from John Smith's youth. Are you a singer yourself?

JS I was. I used to sing at the Mods, the local Gaelic festivals. I didn't speak Gaelic myself. Gaelic had died out largely in mid-Argyll where I was brought up although my mother has quite a lot of Gaelic but we learnt the words and we sang in the Gaelic choirs and things like that. I actually won a medal once for singing at a local Mod.

SL And do you still sing now?

JS Yes, I'm known to break into Gaelic songs. Late into the night.

SL Your childhood sounds nothing short of idyllic really. You were born in a remote island village, on the shores of a loch, your grandfather a fisherman and your father the local schoolmaster. Was it as romantic as it sounds?

JS I think it was a very happy place to be brought up. I think there's a lot to be said for small villages. They are not all peaceful, I mean there are tremendous battles of personalities going on and people who haven't been brought up in a small village don't sometimes understand that, but it was in the countryside, it was near the sea, I was mad on boats and I enjoyed that very much. I had a slight problem being the schoolmaster's son because there were sort of major figures in the village and they were the schoolmaster, the doctor and the minister and you were marked out slightly for being that but the great thing about it was that you were very close with everybody. There was no class-consciousness or divisions and there was a sense of unity about the place. Ardrishaig which is at one end of the Crinan Canal where the Crinan Canal goes from Loch Fyne right through to the Western Isles. I enjoyed it and I think it was a good home to be brought up in. A sort of mixture of radicalism and Christianity which I think was quite an important influence on me. But I left home at quite an early age because we were such a small place, there wasn't a school after the age of 14, so I went off and stayed at lodgings to go to school.

SL What, all by yourself?

JS Yes, by myself in a place called Dunoon. I went to Dunoon Grammar School.

SL How far away was that?

JS It as about 60 or 70 miles but it meant that you were effectively away from home in term-time and you just came back home at Christmas and . . .

SL So you had a landlady and a little room and you took yourself off to school every day?

JS Yes, that was always a bit sad. On the other hand, I suppose it encouraged independence.

SL No home sickness or anything?

JS I didn't have any – no. I was actually quite glad to go. I don't want to put that too crudely to my parents but I enjoyed the independence and the freedom.

SL Your second record?

JS *The Easter Hymn* from *Cavellaria Rusticana*. This, I think, was the first opera that I found I enjoyed and I understood it as it has a very basic plot, I understood it and I thought it was just so beautiful that I felt I would have to take this with me to my desert island.

SL Tell me about university, John? Glasgow, where you read History and Law, but you had joined the Labour Party by then?

JS Yes, I had. I joined the Labour Party when I was in school when I was 16 and I was involved a little bit in political activity at school and in the debating society and then I went to Glasgow University and did a History degree. We had a tradition then which I think was quite good in that before you did a Law degree you did a general degree so that you were properly educated, as it were, before you did Law.

SL So you were there . . . seven years?

JS Yes, seven years, yes, but in the last three years I did an LLB and forbye that there was a year's apprenticeship in a solicitor's office so that you became a qualified solicitor after that period.

SL So you could earn some money after that?

JS Yes, you could, and I did. I wanted to go to the Bar but I couldn't afford to go to the Bar and I had no connections in the Law at all, so I had to become a solicitor for a year or two, which was very good in many ways because it, well, it kept me behind a bit in going to the Bar as early as I wanted. On the other hand I found it very good training but I think the difference between the Bar and solicitors is not quite as wide in Scotland as it is in England.

SL But you had already started developing some skill going towards the Bar because you started debating, this very flourishing club system at university?

JS Glasgow University has always been a great university for debating and its political debating, so it couldn't be designed better for me. I took to it like a duck to water.

SL Did you realise then that you would have to make a choice between the two, politics and the law, eventually?

JS I think I did but I didn't know when and how and these things just resolve themselves. I was a candidate when I was very young, I was a candidate when I was a student at university, at about 23 in a by-election, and eventually I was asked to stand for a seat. It was a pretty safe seat and it was clear to me that if I was elected, then I would become a Member of Parliament. That was in 1969 to 1970, so cutting short, I suppose, my legal career.

SL So you always knew, did you, that when it came to the crunch you would choose politics and not the law?

JS Yes I would have been disappointed, I think, if I had not got into politics and I think if I had got flung out of Parliament I wouldn't be too disconsolate about it as I would just go back to my trade, as it were, go back to the Bar. I suppose it's becoming harder, the longer I was away from it, but certainly in the early years I wasn't worried about that. But I'm glad I went into politics and the only regret that I have in 21 years in Parliament is that 16 of them have been in Opposition – but that's something I hope to put right fairly shortly.

SL What about record three?

JS *Ae Fond Kiss* by Kenneth McKellar. I think Kenneth is a lovely singer and I think this is one of Burns' most beautiful songs. And of course, Burns, apart from being a poet, was a great collector of folk songs and I think Walter Scott said of this one that it was the essence of a thousand love tales. I would like to take that with me to think about on my desert island.

SL You need a lot of money, John, to study for the Bar. It's a lengthy and expensive path. Didn't the General Election of 1966 net you the wherewithal?

JS Yes, well, I was helped a bit because I put some shrewd wagers on and we discovered, some chums and I, that the bookies were having evens on the Conservatives to lose seats under 5,000. But it was clear there was a Labour swing going on so we found a seat which we thought might be lost, even by the Scottish Conservatives, and we put some money on it and then we were affected by our conscience on that one, that we shouldn't be betting on the Conservatives so we bet on a Labour victory on another seat in Berwick and East Lothian which I believe John Mackintosh was standing for, and I think we doubled them up together and we netted quite a lot of money from that, and that allowed me the sort of freedom to go both to the Bar and get married at the same time. So it was quite a fortune at the time.

SL My goodness, one has visions of you staggering from the bookmakers with large amounts of money.

JS It wasn't quite like that, but actually the bookmaker put some money on it himself because when he saw we were quite keen on it he thought we knew what we were doing. But politics can sometimes turn out like that.

SL But, as you say, in 1970 it was, you entered Parliament from North Lanark. You mentioned that you spent 16 of your 21 years in politics in Opposition. That must be the most enormous frustration for a man who obviously considers himself able. Politics apart, do you have a sense of personal waste?

JS I don't think so. I think I perhaps ought to have, but I don't have cause. I'm very frustrated in the Opposition. I find it temperamentally very difficult because I want to do things and I enjoyed very much being in Government and the contrast between the two is very stark indeed. On the other hand Opposition is very important to our democratic life. It's very important that there is an alternative, there's an argument and that there's a debate. I suppose one is performing a very important constitutional role by putting Ministers on the spot and seeing them come and seeing them go, as I've seen quite a number come and go, but I really must confess that I would find it difficult to stay too long in Opposition because I hanker after having the opportunity to change things. After all that is why one is in politics, to see that things are changed for the better, to see some of the ideas you believe in put into practice and in Opposition all you do is criticise and hold alternatives without having the chance to prove that they can work.

SL It was said that Jim Callaghan saw you as a future leader. Did he disclose this to you?

JS No, he never put it in those terms. He encouraged me greatly, though, and gave me my first chance in the Cabinet at the age of 40 which was quite a sobering responsibility. I remember the first day I went to the Department it suddenly hit me that I couldn't just write memos to my superiors any longer.

SL You were it.

JS I was it and, sort of, the buck stops there. I think that Jim would be far too careful to say that anyone would be a leader. He was very shrewd and canny in that respect.

SL People, of course, speculate today on you being a potential Labour Leader. I know you feel that the Party has a perfectly good one already but why do you think it is that Neil Kinnock constantly runs behind his own Party in the polls?

JS Because most Leaders of the Opposition do. It's extremely difficult for a Leader of the Opposition to run ahead of his Party. A Prime Minister will normally run ahead of the Government because he or she is in action all the time, they are doing things, they are demonstrating things and the Leader of the Opposition is really one of the most unenviable jobs in any political system in the world.

SL If the next election is lost would you stand as Party Leader?

JS Well, his policies are quite different from any that I might have. I think he is quite a courageous man and of quite a strong character and that's why I think he would make an excellent Prime Minister. If for some reason or another the Leader of the Labour Party became vacant, I would consider standing for that but I must say I'm not driven by some sense that you have to be the Leader of a Party or become Prime Minister of a country to have a valid political life. I used to wonder, I mean, Rab Butler, if you read his book, was always sort of, kind of, disappointed that he never became Prime Minister and if you think of all the things that he did, why on earth he wanted to be disappointed, I don't know. I think it is quite enough to play an important role in the political life of your country without having to become the Leader.

SL You would settle for John Smith, Exchequer.

JS I would, personally, yes.

SL Look what happened to the last man who said that. Shall we have some more music?

JS I would like to have *The Prisoner's Song* from *Fidelio*, the only song from an opera that Beethoven wrote.

SL Tell me about the heart attack, John. October 1988. I'm sure you recall it in every awful detail.

JS Yes, vividly. It was a Sunday and I wasn't feeling very well but I didn't think I was going to have a heart attack. It was my wife, actually, who spotted that everything wasn't quite as it should be. I didn't have any classic symptoms either but she got a neighbour who was a doctor and he took me into the hospital. I went to Edinburgh Royal Infirmary and I sat in the Casualty Department while he ran off to get a doctor to come and see me. I was given a portable electro-cardiogram and it produced a print out and the young doctor who checked it and looked at it said, 'I think you are all right but come and see me later', and as I was dressing to go and see him I just conked out. I just collapsed on the floor. When I next came to, I was on the trolley going into the intensive care unit.

SL But you were in the right place at the right time.

JS Yes, I couldn't have been in a better place at the time. I think within minutes I was in the intensive care unit. I was very fortunate.

SL Things might have been quite different.

JS One doesn't know, I have no way of knowing and try not to think too much about it but yes, I was fortunate at the time. But it's not an experience I would like to go through again.

SL What you didn't do, what you might have done at that stage, is give up politics. Did you consider that?

JS Oh, you have to in that circumstance and I thought about it quite a lot. I thought, would I be fit to do it and do I want to do it? I could have walked away if I had any doubts about it. I thought about it very carefully and I talked about it with my family and we all felt that it was what I really wanted to do and my doctor said I would be fine and it's turned out that way, so I was very happy I recovered and was able to carry on in politics.

SL But how differently do you lead your life now? I mean, you are a calorie counter for a start.

JS Yes, I've got to be more careful about that and I'm interested in exercise and that. But that's been good, it's been positive.

SL Do you still drive yourself as hard? Do you still stay up late at night and get up early next morning?

JS I try not to. What I have done is cut down moving around the country as much as I was doing. I still do incredible things like train journeys changing at Crewe to get somewhere else. I'm very bad at saying no to go to do things that I thought were needed to be done. I would criss-cross the country and I'm much more careful about that now and that's far more sensible in any event as I haven't lost very much by it.

SL It is nevertheless a shock to discover that you are not indestructible when you presumed you had been, over the years?

JS You feel very vulnerable lying in a hospital bed all wired up and people obviously concerned about what happens. It's much worse for others. My wife turned up at the hospital and they told her, we'll tell you in half an hour whether he is going to survive or not. That's much worse than, in a sense, being the victim.

SL Your next piece of music, the fifth piece?

JS Well, Country and Western. *I've Loved and Lost Again* by Patsy Cline. I like Country and Western music and my daughters are devoted to it. We used to play it in the car when the family went around and we learnt the words and we all sang them together as the tape played in the car, so I have very happy family memories associated with it.

SL You mention exercise, hill climbing. Don't you suffer from a very Scottish disease from which there is no known cure called Munrosis?

JS Yes, Munro bagging. It's very bad, I have an almost terminal condition by it. Where you have got the ambition to climb as many as possible. There are 277 Munros classified by Sir Hugh Munro a hundred years ago this year, when he classified hills above 3,000 feet that stood as separate and independent mountains. There's a rather subjective judgement as to which ones are the Munros but they are accepted by the walking and climbing fraternity and you try and do as many as you can.

SL And how many have you climbed?

JS I've done 69 so far.

SL And there are 277?

JS Yes, I've got quite a lot to do, as you can gather from that.

SL But it's walking, it's not rock climbing.

JS No, it's not climbing at all, in fact I wouldn't dare climb. It's really hill walking in lonely desolate country, but I love it. I like the exercise, I like getting up to the peaks and I love the desolation and the feeling of remoteness. Which is very important. I think the Highlands are one of the few parts of Europe that are genuinely kind of lonely country, where you can walk for days without seeing people, and I enjoy it very much indeed. It's this mixture of beautiful scenery, the feeling of being detached and also good exercise which I think is a winning combination.

SL You are obviously, though, a man who likes goals and tasks and achievements. You are gregarious, as you say. You're going to have a terrible time on a desert island, aren't you?

JS Terrible. I mean I would try to escape from day one. I would be plotting my way out of it and trying to work my way out because I would find the loneliness terrible. I think I would sunbathe for the first few days and I think that would be quite good fun.

156

SL You're not, I suspect, much of a shelter knocker-upper?

JS I don't think so, no. I would concentate on building a boat to get away and have a shot at it.

SL And you could fish 'cause your grandad must have taught you that?

JS He was a herring fisherman. He fished with nets but I can actually, I used to when I was a boy be able to. I think that would come back to me and I would manage to survive on fish.

SL So survival, but with a strong emphasis on escape?

JS Oh, as soon as possible, get away, yes.

SL Your next piece of music, please.

JS Bruch's Violin Concerto Number One in G Minor.

SL The Labour Party were, I'm sure, John, looking forward to a General Election with Mrs Thatcher and with the Poll Tax. Both of these foxes have now been shot. That alone makes the task much more difficult but isn't your fundamental problem one of convincing the electorate that you could do it? That the Labour Party was capable after all those years in Opposition, of running the country.

JS I think that's a task for all political parties in all circumstances and, of course, you are right in saying that it's a special obligation on a party that's been in Opposition for some time. Although I think we are succeeding, and we are assisted greatly of course with the incompetence of, especially, the present administration, particularly in the field of economics, and we wouldn't have to be too ambitious to say that we could handle things a little bit different than they did. But it is certainly there, and the credibility of a political party and of its programme and the people who would be administering the programme are crucial in a democratic decision.

SL And people are therefore sceptical about your plans, economically speaking, of your plans and your promises and they don't know whether to believe your mathematics or not.

JS I think it's the proper attitude to take, for an electorate to be sceptical about politics. I never object to that. That's a challenge for me to persuade them that their scepticism is not justified, but it's a very good starting point and it's an intelligent and mature democracy that says, well prove it to me, persuade me and show me you can do it. Now it's a good testing process and it's good for politicians, too, to go through that.

SL But again, has John Major not shot your foxes as Chancellor of the Exchequer? I mean, you were talking about entry into the ERM which he has done, you were talking about bringing down interest rates which has happened. The Poll Tax has gone. In a sense, to mix the metaphors, your clothes have been stolen.

JS No, we've got plenty clothes but imitation is the sincerest form of flattery and we are right about a number of things, but they have had to understand that and accept that.

SL Again, phrases like 'world-class economy', 'a fairer and better society', 'a well-trained and educated workforce' – in a sense you are calling for the same thing, it's just the methods that are different.

JS Well, we know from what has happened in the last ten years from a number of these things that we are far from a world-class economy. We now have an economy which is bottom of the European league, but most of all in education and training we have slipped behind the rest of Europe, and if there is one thing that I am absolutely determined in at least playing some part in doing, is help create the best-educated and well-trained workforce in Europe. I mean, this links me back to my past, to the schoolhouse. I suppose I was intoxicated by education and I suppose Scots carry it with them easily. But I really do want to see that done and see that this is a country that we can say, after ten years, whatever else is right or wrong here, this is the place where young people can go as far as they can and as far as their abilities take them and as far as they want to go, and that this is a land of true opportunity.

SL Next record?

JS *The Road to the Isles* sung by Father Sidney McEwan. It's an old recording, it goes back to the 1930s, but I knew Father Sidney McEwan very well. He was the Catholic Priest at Lochgilphead, the nearest town to the one I lived in and he was a marvellous man. I used to look after his boat, actually, as a boy. But he was a Catholic Priest in a very Presbyterian part of the country and he was a very well liked man and also a very beautiful singer and I would like to have my memories of my childhood confirmed by listening to him.

SL There's obviously a sentimental side to John Smith which the public doesn't very often get to see. Do you consciously hide it?

JS No, I don't consciously hide it, but I just don't have occasion to show it. But I think I am really quite badly sentimental.

SL And what about the folk of your native village? Do they get to see anything of their famous son these days?

JS Yes, occasionally. They often write to me with problems. They think if you come from Argyll you are there to solve them and I've got to write diplomatically that they have their own Member of Parliament but that's the style. I remember when I became Secretary of State for Trade and I was responsible for merchant shipping, a local fisherman wrote to me and said, now that you are Secretary of State for Trade, John, you can sort out the accident I had with the boat when it hit the pier. The Civil Servants in the Department were very puzzled as to how to reply so I took that one away from them and said I would reply to that one myself as I didn't think they would handle it with sufficient tact.

SL If you set out from that village again now, aged 18 and going off to university, would you do it any different the second time out?

JS No, I don't think so. I have been very fortunate in having had, so far anyway, a fairly exciting, adventurous life, and I've made many, many good friends. On the whole, I've enjoyed the voyage and I don't think I would change a single thing.

SL That's a big thing to be able to say. I mean you must therefore class yourself as a very lucky man?

JS Extraordinarily fortunate. Not just in terms of surviving illness but also in terms of having a happy family and having a very enjoyable life, and working at what I wanted to do and feeling secure is very important. I think it starts off, in a sense, if you are brought up in a happy family and then you try to create one yourself, and I don't know whether we have done that or not but we have certainly tried. I enjoy politics and I enjoy the camaraderie of politics and I also think I am engaged in something quite important. I think I need to feel it's important and worth putting effort into and is also for the benefit of others.

SL We end with Mozart, I think?

JS Yes, well, Mozart is just the most splendid of all composers and the Mozart operas are the greatest joys of my life to listen to and I'd like to have a piece from near the end of *The Marriage of Figaro*.

SL So which one of the eight will you need most then?

JS Mozart, that's the one I would take, without any hesitation.

SL No island is complete without him. A book?

JS I would like to take an anthology of poems because I think poems can be read over and over again and anything else that you read, if it's a novel you've sort of got the story I think in a sense, but poems, and a great variety of them in an anthology.

SL Through the ages?

JS Yes, oh yes.

SL And a luxury?

JS I would take a case of champagne. I would enjoy drinking it and then I would send messages out in the bottles.

159

JOHN SMITH

YOUR CANDIDATE FOR THE

70s

POLLING DAY
THURSDAY, 18th JUNE, 1970
7 a.m. — 10 p.m.

FACE The FUTURE WITH
CONFIDENCE
VOTE LABOUR

JOHN SMITH your Labour Candidate is 31 years of age and is an advocate by profession. John and his wife, Elizabeth, have a daughter, Sarah, aged 18 months. He was educated at Dunoon Grammar School and Glasgow University where he graduated M.A. and LL.B. He was a solicitor in Glasgow before being called to the Scottish Bar in 1967. An active member of the Labour Party since his schooldays, John fought the 1961 by-election in East Fife for Labour at the age of 23 and fought there again in 1964.

John Smith is proud to represent Labour in the North Lanarkshire Constituency and offers his ability, vigour and idealism for your service in the great tradition set by Margaret Herbison.

John Smith, your candidate for the '70s

On holiday on the Island of Eigg, 1987

On holiday in Iona, 1978, with Jane, Catherine and Sarah

*Visiting a gun emplacement in the Golan Heights,
Israel, 1993*

*Lunch at the Sea of Galilee with Catherine, Jane, Elizabeth
and Sarah*

Buachaille Etive Mor, September 1992

John Smith and Murray Elder

John Smith with Prince Charles at Willie Brandt's funeral
(© S.J. Darchinger IFJ/Marc Darchinger)

The Rt. Hon. John Smith QC, MP speaking at the River
Club, Monday, 16 April 1990

The Labour Shadow Cabinet at Westminster, July 1992
(© PA Photo Library)

Brighton Party Conference, 1993
(© Universal Pictorial Press)

The leadership election, with Catherine, Elizabeth, Jane and Sarah, July 1992

A moment of quiet contemplation (© London Daily News)

Part Three

Press and Public Tributes

Press Tributes

Literally dozens of tributes to John Smith appeared in the world's press after his death. This section features just five of these and we are grateful to the journalists and proprietors of the relevant newspapers for permission to reproduce the articles.

The Last British Statesman

by

Neal Ascherson

'The people know that they have lost a friend.' Donald Dewar said it, in the Cluny Church in Edinburgh. As a Glasgow Labour MP, close to John Smith for a lifetime, he chose his words well. Outside the church, the crowd standing in the icy spring wind heard him, and stirred a little. That was why they were there.

Britain does not go in for political funerals. When Wellington and Churchill were carried through the streets, the people came to remember past glories and old victories. The idea that a funeral can be not only a farewell but a new beginning is a foreign one. But the death of John Smith has released a strange, very fresh gust of feeling. Like the cold wind blowing over Morningside from the sea, it carries a faint scent of something forgotten and remote: faith in a leader and trust in what he stood for. They carried John Smith's coffin carefully down the steps to the hearse. A few people in the crowd wiped their eyes; most remained impassive, their faces closed. The Prime Minister and his wife emerged into silence. So did the politicians who followed: old Michael Foot being helped down the steps, Tony Blair walking alone in a space between his party comrades. Questioned, people said reluctantly that John Smith had been an honest man, not proud, a man who listened to ordinary folk and who should have led the country.

It was a Scottish occasion. In the church, there was little ritual; God was praised, but mostly for helping 'a good and brave man' to fight for the happiness of others. The minister said: 'He did justice, he loved mercy, he walked humbly with his God.' This was not what we are used to hearing about politicians. And, equally unexpected, the speakers seemed to rejoice in John Smith's achievement, rather than mourn for a life brutally cut off on what might have been the threshold of triumph.

Scotland is a nation inured to disappointment, to defeats snatched from the jaws of victory. But this did not feel like one more 'what might

165

have been' calamity. John Smith, suddenly, showed people that there was a style of politics, a type of politician with which they could identify. He had seemed at first bustling, ambitious, lawyerly – much like the rest of them. But then his quality began to reach through. It was seen that he was high spirited but also that he was angry about selfishness and unfairness, that he meant what he said. We in the media missed this secret change in public opinion. So much the worse for us.

John Smith was more than half-way across the bridge to glory when he fell. To die at such a moment of promise is tragic, and yet the mourners in Edinburgh did not feel that the world was utterly unfair and impossible. The 'lost leader' bitterness was somehow missing. It was as if the dead man had unlocked a rusty gate, so that a way ahead was open. An Edinburgh councillor, standing with her children, said, 'When I go round the doorsteps, they say: "you're all the same". So where does this feeling come from?'

It comes from a sort of relief. The British, perhaps for a moment only, are tired of their own superficial cynicism about politics, and when John Smith died it suddenly seemed unbearable to lump him with 'all the others'. The gate has opened to anyone who can carry on what John Smith began: restoring self-respect to people who still have values but no longer know what to do with them. For him, these values were the sort of practical, capable, non-ideological attack on greed and privilege, in the name of morality and efficiency, which the British have often supported.

Watching the coffin go, a friend in the crowd said: 'That was the last British statesman.' He meant that no future leader would be comfortable – as Smith would have been comfortable – to be at once Scottish and British and Prime Minister at Westminster. John Smith loved Scotland extravagantly, and his most important unfinished business was the establishment of a Scottish parliament within the UK. He was convinced that this would strengthen the Union, and begin the reform – the 'Europeanisation' – of the British state. His successors may be less confident.

Today, he is being buried on the island of Iona. Most Scots are moved and comforted by this decision. It salutes John Smith's romantic, Highland side.

But it is also a statement. His Christian socialism arises from Argyll, whose ruined villages write a very simple message on the landscape about what the uncontrolled strong will do to the unprotected weak. John Smith tried to make a weary, declining industrial society read this message and recover enough confidence to act on it. When he died, the British had been warming to him, whether they will act, we shall see.

The Independent,
21 May 1994

166

The Man Who Would Have Led Britain

by

Andrew Marr

The greatest political tribute to John Smith is the simplest one: had he lived, he would have become Prime Minister. That is a guess, of course, an assertion thrown into the darkness. But over the past few months I, like many others, had slowly come round to the belief that the likeliest outcome of the next election was a Labour victory. This was not only because of Conservative disunity. It was because of the will and the worth of Mr Smith.

For they – we – got him wrong. The London-based political classes never quite understood this man. They were prepared to concede his decency and seriousness, to mutter about lawyers, Presbyterianism and Scottish Sunday afternoons, to grant him the odd good joke across the despatch box.

But they seemed almost blind to his huge and mounting popularity in the country – opinion-poll ratings rivalled only by Harold Wilson at the height of his radical reputation in the Sixties. Labour MPs such as Dennis Skinner were reporting extraordinary events – 650 people turning up at meetings in small cathedral towns. Something was happening in Britain, even if Westminster had barely noticed. That something was Mr Smith, in his certainty, making contact.

This is not an easy country, nor an easy time, for political leadership. The failure of so many familiar nostrums has left an uncertain people, suspicious of promises and temperamentally ready for betrayal. To them, Mr Smith had been sending quite quiet, consistent and unrhetorical messages. He was quite sure he would win. He was quite sure he could help.

This is a time in which democratic leaders are raised high, then savagely brought down, a grim carnival of grotesques. But Mr Smith was self-confident enough to disappear from view, to stay almost comically ordinary, to give others the credit. He never struck attitudes or sought attention for himself. Faced by the media demanding instant policy, a political agenda subservient to the news agenda, he was infuriatingly passive. He was keeping his eye on the long-term, thank you. It was conventional, unheroic and frankly, we thought, a little simplistic. But it was working.

Yes, we got him wrong. We did not look closely enough. What was precious and rare in him was his anger. This may seem an odd judgement on a man known for his good humour, wit and zest for life. But it did not take long when one had him by himself for the conversation to turn to the unfashionable matter of poverty. He thought about the lives of his poorer and unemployed constituents and the effect on him was almost eerie. He would start on what it was like to live on benefits as a single mother. His voice would harden and suddenly you found that the easy-going Westminster Good Old Boy you thought you were sitting next to had disappeared and you were making eye-contact with someone you hadn't realised was in the room – a driven, angry and quietly implacable soul.

Serious? Oh yes. Scottish serious. Those policy 'mistakes' – his insistence on a national minimum wage, the Social Charter, the requirement in 1992 for higher taxes on middle-income families, were at the core of his political meaning, his old-fashioned Christian anger. For a man of the Labour right, the essence of respectability, Mr Smith was curiously popular and admired by those Labour left-wingers who knew him well.

His tax policies may have helped Labour lose the 1992 election and would have been finessed before the next one. He was too focused on winning to make the same mistake twice. But Prime Minister Smith would have surprised the middle-class South (a part of the nation I think he never really understood). However reassuringly conventional the suit and spectacles, when he used words like fairness, opportunity, greed, he meant them. Some would have been shocked by the results; others, perhaps, inspired.

As almost every tribute has mentioned, he was a witty man, warm and painstaking in small acts of kindness. I will never forget the small flicker of pleasure when I turned a Commons corridor and saw that short, bulky form approaching – fast walk, alert gaze, sharp comment still. I won't forget staring down into the Commons chamber and getting an unexpected wink and broad grin from him. I won't forget the laughter, infectious as flu, or the unrepeatable jokes.

But none of that is really the story of what has gone. I contend that the reason why Mr Smith connected to voters was that they somehow saw through the cheery but cautious Westminster man, and grasped a little of the steeliness, the anger, and the general grown-upness of the politician behind. They saw a man most politicians didn't. You may call that romanticism, or the emotion of the moment. But this is the day for emotion. We are missing someone special. We are missing a version of the future, a human chance that has gone.

THE MAN WHO WOULD HAVE LED BRITAIN

He is the lost leader of a lost country. Had he lived, he would have entered our lives, affected our wealth, altered our morale, changed how we thought about our country, influenced the education of our children. His grin would have become a familiar icon, his diction the raw material of satire. At however many removes, and however obscurely, his personality would have glinted through the state and touched us all. For good or ill? The question is now meaningless. That Britain won't happen.

The Independent,
13 May 1994

He Was Witty, He Was Bright and Could Spot Fools at Ten Paces!

by

Helen Liddell

The world has lost a great political leader, but how to tell what it feels like to lose a friend? A man proud beyond belief of his clever, vivacious and intelligent family, John beamed when Elizabeth came in to any room. The father of one of the happiest families in British politics, one of the proudest husbands.

Only a few weeks ago, John's brother-in-law died. Now grief again has hit the family. All of us who share it cannot understand what has happened. He was witty, he was bright, he had an appalling temper and could spot a fool at ten paces. During the last election we travelled the country by helicopter. I would be sick, he would pass the sick bag. We passed the time counting the swimming pools of the south of England. It was the weather we envied, not the riches.

The man I first met 20 years ago was never the sober, puritanical figure of his public image. He was great fun, he loved a laugh and he had a wealth of stories. Many of them were very near the bone. He loved to talk about his days at the Bar. He never passed Barlinnie without doffing an imaginary cap at the home of so many of his former clients.

Politicians kiss babies. We expect it of them, John Smith hugged them, cuddled them, threatened to take them home. In a house in Blackpool as the local party lined up in the good frocks and the Sunday suits, John body-swerved the lot and made for a two-year-old. Not a photographer in sight. And cats, he loved them. Shelly, the tiger in disguise, who yesterday sat in the window waiting for his master to come home, was spoiled rotten.

No dinner table was complete without John. He brought excitement and wit to even sausage and chips. He loved food, he liked a drink, but latterly with an eye to his health.

If a friend asked a favour, he could not say no. In October 1988 I invited him to a dinner at the Labour Party conference. He already had four other invitations, but he would not turn me down. We had coffee together, he had one course with each of his other hosts. A few days later, he had his first heart attack.

John the common man in Airdrie market was a sight to behold. Anger sometimes bubbled near the surface. He could be difficult, but never more so than when he was confronted with poverty. A favourite story was about a single parent in Plains working her fingers to the bone to give her daughter the training she needed to become an opera singer. He could not understand why no one would help her. He was a man of values. The old-fashioned kind. A dedicated Christian, but never a Holy Willie, his beliefs guided his politics.

A favourite memory of mine is of a Labour Party conference in Dunoon, when one of the stewards in the local party, by his demeanour clearly a former headmaster, asked me with pride if I knew his son. Of course I knew John Smith QC, MP, member of Her Majesty's Government, one of the brightest minds of his generation.

In Tighnabruaich, Andrew Irvine and Son is the local draper. There will be mourning there today. The young John boarded with the grandmother of the present Andrew Irvine when he was a pupil at Dunoon Grammar. John spoke often of the Irvines. He never forgot a kindness.

In the hallway of John's Edinburgh house with the memorabilia of a lifetime in politics there is a picture of the last Labour Government taken in No 10. John is second from the left standing behind a seated Tony Benn. As I left his house in the early hours of the morning after the last election when Labour had failed yet again he tapped that picture and vowed: 'One day we'll be back.'

Yes Labour will be back. But without one of its greatest leaders and kindest men.

Daily Record,
13 May 1994

John Smith's Great Journey

by

Alastair Campbell

How quickly, and how cruelly, can dreams be dashed. Just after nine o'clock on Wednesday night, John Smith stood before an audience of colleagues, supporters and businessmen, and vowed to lead Labour to victory at the European elections and beyond. Twelve hours later, he was dead. Aged 55.

I cannot recall a political death which has provoked such sadness at Westminster. Across the parties. Amongst the policemen, the journalists, the canteen staff. John Smith was a Westminster man, and it was not just the Labour Party that was mourning him there yesterday.

Alongside Smith as he spoke at Wednesday's gala dinner to raise funds for Labour's European elections was French Socialist Party leader Michel Rocard, guest speaker. The two men were friends. Smith painted a picture of the day when Rocard was running France, their mutual friend Rudolf Scharping was running Germany and Smith was running Britain. One day, he vowed, the whole of Europe might be run by democratic socialist governments. It was the dream that drove him on.

Several times during his speech, as he had done in many speeches before, he stressed the twin pillars of his beliefs – economic efficiency and social justice. To some, they are slogans, chanted by Labour politicians down the years. To Smith, they were the very reasons for his being.

He had an intense belief in right and wrong, instilled by a strict but loving Presbyterian upbringing, and an almost evangelical loathing of poverty. He was intensely Scottish. I recall a party, at a time when what he called 'the London papers' were criticising him for promoting too many Scots to senior jobs. 'There's no such thing as too many Scots,' he insisted.

He defied conventional wisdoms, and delighted in doing so. 'Ach' was one of his favourite words. It was a way of dismissing 'fancy notions'. It was a stance born of supreme self-confidence. That, in turn, was born of the depth of his political convictions, a sharp intellect and a tight-knit circle of close friends formed in his days as a Glasgow University student and a Scottish QC. Chief among those friends were Donald Dewar, the MP, and Derry Irvine, now Lord Irvine, a lawyer.

Above all, that self-confidence was born of a secure and loving family environment. He was as devoted to his wife Elzabeth, and to his three daughters, as they were to him. Visitors to his comfortable, very middle-class, very Edinburgh home, were struck by the banter between them, three very modern young women who clearly adored a seemingly old-fashioned father.

He *was* old-fashioned in many ways, and saw no reason to apologise for it. He was, above all, a man of integrity. That too was a theme of Wednesday's speech, as he explained why he was so angry that Social Security Minister Nicholas Scott has refused to resign over the wrecking of a Bill to help the disabled. 'This is about standards in public life,' he said.

Nobody ever doubted Smith's standards. Politics to him was a moral calling. Of his many memorable speeches in the Commons, the one that stands out for me was his response to last year's Queen's Speech.

It was *wrong* to cut sick pay. It was *wrong* to raise national insurance. The Government's treatment of the poor was *wrong*. Many politicians, when they speak of right and wrong, are unconvincing. But right and wrong were key words in John Smith's personal and political vocabulary.

Nobody ever doubted his socialism. Always on the right of the party, he was never afraid to use the word socialist. Yet he valued loyalty, and was never tempted to join the exodus of leading right-wingers to the SDP, preferring to stay and fight his corner.

He was always confident that Labour would shed the policies that he felt damaged the party in recent elections – on defence, on crime, on the economy. He took immense pride in the way that the Labour Party had turned tax and crime, two of the party's historic weaknesses, into issues on which they now enjoy a poll lead. His unwavering stance on such issues won him the respect of the left as well as the right wing he had always represented. It meant that when Neil Kinnock resigned following election defeat in 1992, Smith was the obvious successor. And he trounced challenger Bryan Gould by nine to one.

Again returning to that speech on Wednesday evening, which at the time was seen by some in the audience as being over long, but which now will be remembered as his own political obituary, he was big enough to thank John Major and the Tories for the help they had given him in establishing a huge opinion poll lead. But that lead was also at least in part explained by him, and by his leadership of the party.

He paid tribute in his speech to Neil Kinnock, in the specific context of his predecessor's fight against apartheid. The two men were never close. Party leaders and their Chancellors and Shadow Chancellors rarely are. But they had a great deal of regard for each other's abilities. Neil Kinnock saved the Labour Party from itself, and from possible extinction.

John Smith was emerging as the leader who would finally win the trust of the British people, the trust required to get into office. It was easy to imagine Smith in Downing Street. He was a creature of Government. He served briefly in the last Labour Cabinet, as Trade Secretary – the only member of the current Shadow Cabinet to have done so. 'I don't enjoy Opposition,' he once told me. 'You don't go into politics to be in Opposition. Where's the sense in that?'

He believed passionately in parliamentary democracy. One of the criticisms which would meet an 'Ach' response was the suggestion that he worried too much about his performances in Parliament, and less about life outside.

Yet he was a vigorous campaigner, not least during the recent local elections campaign, prompting his wife Elizabeth to worry that he had been pushing himself too hard. A worry she confided to health spokesman David Blunkett at Wednesday's Park Lane Hotel dinner.

But Parliament was the key to his success. Successive senior Cabinet Ministers suffered at the hands of his wit and his analysis of economic policy. Though he found the theatre of Prime Minister's Questions irritating, he regularly got the better of the Prime Minister. Nor did it upset him too much if the Prime Minister got the better of him from time to time. 'Ach, you win some, you lose some.' His innate caution had led to fears of complacency, a belief that Labour was simply relying on the Government to destroy itself. Smith did, however, have a strategy, one which saw his party causing maximum difficulty for the Tories, devising final policies late in the parliament, a short manifesto, and an election campaign which relied heavily on the authority he hoped by then to have established.

That he was doing so is beyond dispute. It is ridiculous to claim he was a great leader, in the historic sense, in that he had not been in the job long enough. But that he stood a very fair chance of being the next prime minister was clear. More important, he had a clear idea of what he wanted to do when he got there. It was clear to anyone who heard the speech he made on becoming leader of the Labour Party in 1992.

'Today we are embarking on a great journey', he said, 'a journey to eliminate poverty, injustice and homelessness; a journey to build lasting sustainable prosperity; a journey to persuade millions of the strength of our vision, the relevance of our policies, the urgency of our demand for change and to make Labour the party of government in this country again; a journey that, to succeed, will require tough decisions, unity of purpose, willingness to discard what is wrong.'

He said much the same in that final speech on Wednesday, which I now feel privileged to have heard. He put education and training above all else. He said he wanted people to look back on a Labour Government

. . . 'after ten years, 15 maybe, and say that whatever they might think of us, at least we did the best by our young people. We gave them a chance to fulfil their potential.' All delivered with that sincerity that was the hallmark of his oratory. He had the stillest eyes I have ever seen. They never flickered. He rarely blinked. Yet how often did those eyes fill with laughter.

And now they are closed for ever, while the eyes of so many others fill with tears for their lost leader.

Today,
13 May 1994

One of the Best Loved and Most Admired Scotsmen

by

Ruth Wishart

There were those who complained occasionally about John Smith's energy. Shouldn't he be a bit more visible, be seen to be doing more to damage the Government? And then you wondered if maybe they all had a collective case of mistaken identity on their hands. John Smith was never anything other than formidably energetic.

A couple of weeks ago I popped in to see the family when he was bedridden with badly sprained ligaments. Typically, he was surrounded by papers, fulminating about missing the planned launch of Labour's local election campaigns. He hobbled downstairs to chat to Elizabeth and the girls but almost immediately switched on *The World At One* to catch Margaret Beckett. Then, he called his office in London to discuss tactics. If John Smith was idle in pursuit of success for his party it was a strange kind of indolence. He wanted power for all the unfashionable reasons . . . to bring back equality of opportunity, to restore some of the virtues which underpinned his own unshakeable morality.

Ironically, it was John Smith, more than any other politician I have known, who knew exactly which basics he wanted his country to come back to.

They mocked his bank managerial mode at times; the overtly Presbyterian tone of some of his speeches. But his beliefs were the rock on which he built his life and his home as well as his career. Almost uniquely in his trade he was beyond corruption.

I once asked Elizabeth why, after so many less than lucrative years in opposition, he continued to turn down the offers which came tumbling in from companies and institutions throughout the city. He couldn't possibly risk it, she said. He wouldn't know for sure how they conducted their business. Yesterday, the word integrity was used constantly about John Smith. And it was no accident that it sprang to so many lips.

But the commentators were also unanimous in suggesting that the Labour leadership had brought him no particular airs and graces; no inclination to distance himself from the friendly banter of colleagues, or his usual friends.

There were at least four good reasons why John never got ideas above his station. To Elizabeth and Sarah, Jane and Catherine he wasn't a former minister or a future prime minister. He was the man they teased unmercifully about his waist line; the man round whom they draped ever more outrageous ties to offset the obligatory pinstripe, the man for whom they bought jokey tartan boxer shorts to celebrate his first speech to conference as Labour leader. He wore them, too.

They would post less than flattering pictures on the fridge to remind him that snacking was not to be recommended for a man not ever built to be lean. When John had his first heart attack in 1988 there was a period when he became evangelical about calorie-counted food and even found low-calorie wine. Happily for those privileged to share his hospitality it was a short-lived phase.

He was the most hospitable of men. Several times in the last few years friends and family gathered for summer parties in his home to celebrate important birthdays in the girls' lives. The last was the best: a twin celebration last summer of John's and Elizabeth's silver wedding and Jane's 21st. The sun shone, the champagne flowed and John paid the most touching personal tribute to the family he loved more than anything else in his life.

They had a horrendous day yesterday. Dealing publicly with what for most of us is a private tragedy when we suffer similar loss. Later, they will take comfort from having had, as a husband or father, one of the most talented, but, more importantly, one of the best loved and most admired Scotsmen of his generation.

The Scotsman,
13 May 1994

Public Tributes

There were hundreds of letters, cards and messages of sympathy received by the Smith family after John Smith's death. They were a source of great comfort and strength. By way of thanks, some of these are reproduced here.

Too Early Yet

by

Kay Stonham

Too early yet to say goodnight
Just as the tide has turned and you're set to win the fight
Just now as grief and failure slip away
Just now before the break of your great day.

Don't leave us while your hopes are young and green
Tormented by a thousand might-have-beens
We never thought to weep for you and mourn
But walk with you towards a kinder dawn.

You've given much to heal and soothe the strife
You've given self and heart and now your life
And though you've helped us to our bright tomorrow
No sweetness in your parting, only sorrow.

read on *Week Ending* 13 May 1994 *BBC Radio* 4

Replied
...

5 Hazelbury Lane
Edmonton
London
N9 9BW
Tel: 081 803 4268

20. 5. 94

Dear Mrs. Smith,

For the whole of
my voting life, (I am now 44),
I had voted Conservative, but
all that changed after Mr.
Smith became leader of the.
Opposition.

It was obvious from the start
that he was a genuine man
who practised what he preached.
I watched with pleasure as he
drew together all facets of the
Labour Party and made it
one – one which was credible
and which I'm sure would

The blessing of the Lord be upon you.

Psalm 129 : 8

have won the next General
Election with ease. I must
admit to being slightly
prejudiced as I am also Scots!
Seriously, however, his death
is a big loss to Britain but
I am quite sure that his
legacy will be the continued
rise of the Labour Party.

As Donald Dewar said,
We have lost a friend."

At this very difficult time,
you and your family will be in
my prayers.

Yours sincerely,

Rachel Wyles.

Replies!
J mol

A. J. MOORE
3 MAES-Y-DRE
GRONANT
PRESTATYN
CLWYD
LL19 9TN

25/5/94

Dear Mrs Smith,

I felt I had to write to you. This may seem strange, as I have been a lifelong Conservative. I basically voted Conservative because I had no confidence in the Labour Party, & felt there wasn't a feasible alternative to the 'Big Two'. I also found the Labour leaders did nothing to inspire me to change my opinions.

All this changed when your husband took up leadership. At last! Someone who made me sit up & take notice. Someone with integrity & foresight, & the ability to change things for the better. Someone I admired, & above all _liked_!

John Smith's leadership wrought a change in me, & in many, many other people —

the Labour Party, & ultimately in the whole country.

It's so sad that he couldn't have lived to reap the fruit from the seeds he sowed — but fruit there will undoubtedly be — & what a personal testimony to a great man.

I too lost my husband to heart disease but my husband also had a massive stroke a year before he died, which robbed him of his speech and mobility. It was tragic, but how much more of a tragedy it would have been if that had happened to the wonderful orator your husband was. He was able to do what he loved doing & to the best of his ability, to the very last day. That is something to be thankful for.

My thoughts and very best wishes to you and your family

Yours sincerely

Audrey J. Moore.

185

Replied
July

Brookfield
Renfrewshire
20TH MAY

Dear Mrs Smith,

Like your beloved husband
John, I was born in 1938 in
Argyll & Bute District, the
daughter of a schoolteacher on
Bute & raised in the
Presbyterian faith, so I
hope you will not mind my
writing these few lines to you
& your family at this sad time.

My husband & I are not
Labour voters, but we had
enormous respect for John
Smith & were humbled by
his caring attitude to the
people of Scotland, & Britain
as a whole. He would

have been a fine Prime
Minister but more important
than that, he was a
wonderful gentleman, and
we send you our deepest
sympathy at this time.
Our own two daughters are
ages with your family & we
all have a deep sense of
loss for "what might have
been". You can be
comforted that so many
share your grief & I'm sure
your private precious memories
will help sustain you and
yours in the days ahead.
With respect,
W.E. Stevenson.

1 BOSWELL CLOSE
HIGH GREEN
SHEFFIELD) S30 4FD
22-5-94.

Dear Mrs Smith,

    I am not politically minded and always looked on politicians has people who promise the world but never delivered. When your husband was made leader I sensed here was a man who was honest and caring and respected the working classes and gave hope for the future.

    I enclose a cheque for £10-00 in lieu of a floral tribute and would ask you to donate it to any organisation or charity of you choice.

    Yours faithfully
    Keith Steele

Words can only help to heal
and let you know
how others feel
that in your time of grief
you can depend
on love and support
from all your friends

With Deepest Sympathy

Keith Steele

Replied
July Mrs Smith

Dear Mrs smith   I liked Mr Smith
because he helped Scotland.

I am eight years old, I live in
Stenhouse mufr

I am very sorry that he died.

by Fraser Duff

Finlaycourt
Stenhousemuir.
            MUIR

Friday 27th May 1991

With
Deepest
Sympathy

To Mrs Smith and family,
with deepest condolences
for the loss of a great man,
from a simple Scot.

Replied
July

Avila,
Balmanno Gardens,
Bridge of Earn,
Perth. PH2 9RH.
7th June 1994

Dear Mrs. Smith, Sarah, Jane & Catherine,

Like so many others who have written to you over recent weeks, I have never met you. However, I feel a great need to write to you and express my deepest sympathy at the death of your husband and father.

I am a final-year Law student at Edinburgh university, and at the time of John's death, I felt so numb that I could not find the words to convey my thoughts and prayers to you all. I then found myself in the midst of my Finals, without the time to write. It is only now that they are over that I feel able to write.

John meant so much to the whole nation. His convictions for what he believed in gave us all a tremendous sense of security and an assurance that somebody was concerned and willing to fight for our welfare. His transformation of the Labour Party over the last two years showed that there is a party worth voting for, and I truly believe that his colleagues are committed to continuing his valuable work.

I am sorry that I never had the honour of meeting John in person. I feel that I knew him so well, however. For the ordinary person like myself, he seemed so easy to relate to, and his love for, and pride in, his family — so evident in everything he said and did — showed that he was the obvious 'father-figure' to lead our country.

Before leaving my flat in Newington to walk over to Cluny Parish Church, on the morning of John's funeral, I learned that I had secured a legal traineeship for when I complete my degree — the first step to fully joining the legal profession. I intend to dedicate my work to John's memory.

He has been and will remain an inspiration to my generation — not only in his work in law and politics, but in his whole life. He has given us the hope and promise of a better future.

I plan to make a trip to Iona in the next few months, to say my own personal farewell to John. I will miss him greatly.

Once again, I want to express my sympathy to you all. Being of a similar age to your daughters, I cannot imagine what the loss of a parent must be like, but hope that your fond memories of John, and the knowledge that we all share your loss, will provide you with some comfort.

Thinking of you all often, and remembering you and John in my prayers.

With love and best wishes,
Miranda Becker

(Age 21 yrs)

Excerpt from Prof. James A. Whyte's sermon at
Hope Park Church, St. Andrews on Sunday 15th
May 1994

"I think of our reaction to the death of John
Smith.

I am now in my mid-70s and I cannot remember
the death of a public figure occasion such
widespread dismay and grief.   In all
political parties they grieved.   Politics,
party conference, campaigning were suspended
while they came to terms with this loss.
And what they mourned, when they came to
express their tributes, was the man of
integrity, the man with no hidden agenda, the
man at ease with himself and with his
fellows, the man with a zest for life and a
passion for the things that ultimately
matter.   And such was his witness, however
imperfect - for no-one embodies these things
perfectly - that people recognised that these
are the things that ultimately matter, and
whether they knew it or not, what they
honoured in this Christian man was the
Lordship of his Master".

sent by Anne Irvine.

To Mrs Smith
You don't
know me but
I drive past
your house
every day &
just want to
wish you well.
Anita Levinson.

Tel. 0708 453435   *Replied* 'Trees'
                    225 Wingletye Lane
                    Hornchurch, Essex.
                    RM11 3BL.
                    31st. May 1994

Dear Mrs Smith and Daughters,

Please forgive me writing so late but I have found it most difficult to put into words, my feelings of deep sadness at the awful sudden death of your dear husband and father. The emotional pain of losing such a very special person has left a deep impression on me, my family, and many millions of others I am sure who have been traumatized by the loss. Never can I remember having been emotionally affected by anyone's death; notwithstanding personal relations; since the assasination of President John F. Kennedy.

A brilliant light has been extinguished and I do believe this country has lost a great man, and a future great prime minister. With his statesmanship, integrity, humility and humour, together with his Christian Family moral and ethical ideals, he would I think, by example, have pulled this country out of the deep melaise into which it seems to have drifted.

Fine words cannot ever I know, replace one's husband and father but the nation's genuine grief shared

...ith you all at the funeral, I hope, would have been ...ne small comfort for your great trauma. Having myself ...atched the funeral on television and hearing all the fine ...ibutes expressed that day, and seeing your devotion and ...gnity, made one feel very humble.

You are quoted as saying, "Everything I've ever done ...s with him, beside him, behind him. He makes us proud ...no finer epitaph could be written for someone so sorely ...missed. I do hope that a fitting memorial to your husband's

In the sadness of the present
may you somehow come to see
that the beauty of the past
remains in loving memory.

memory can be put in place eventually.

Yours in sadness sincerely,

God Bless You and Keep You,

Gerard A. Porter

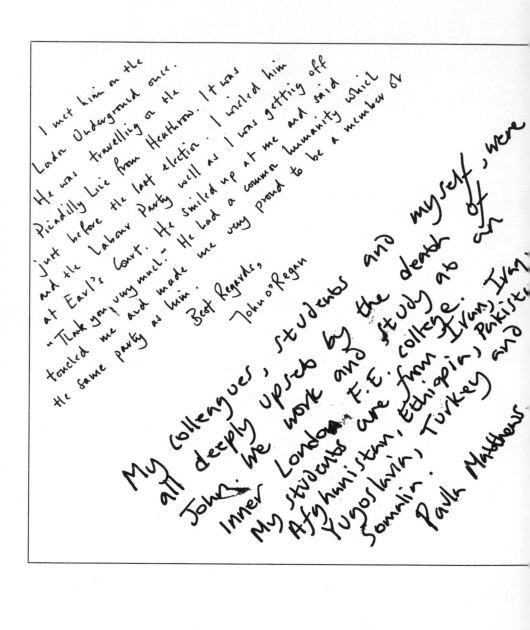

I met him on the London Underground once. He was travelling on the Piccadilly Line from Heathrow. It was just before the last election. I invited him and the Labour Party well as I was getting off at Earl's Court. He smiled up at me and said "Thank you very much." He had a common humanity which touched me and made me very proud to be a member of the same party as him.

Best Regards,
John o'Regan

My colleagues, students and myself, were all deeply upset by the death of John. We work and study at an Inner London F.E. college. Ivan. Ivan, My students are from Ivan, Pakistan Afghanistan, Ethiopia, Pakistan Yugoslavia, Turkey and Somalia.

Paula Matthews

196

Mrs Smith, Sarah, Jane and
Catherine

With sympathy
... thinking of you at this sad time

Best Wishes

Paula Matthews

Tst. S Rijm.

197

Replied
July.

310, Oxgangs Rd. N.
Edinburgh
EH13 9NE
20/5/94

Dear Mrs Smith,

I am sorry I have taken so long to write a brief note of condolence to you & your daughters, but I know you must have been overwhelmed by the many cards & letters you received from very ordinary admirers of your late husband. You & your girls have lost a wonderful loving husband & father, & Scotland has lost a great man of honesty & integrity who would have been our country's finest prime minister.

Be assured this morning you & your daughters will be surrounded by waves of respect & affection from the many ordinary people who will be lining the pavements around Cluny Church to mourn your loss.

I hope your final journey

Together to Iona will be peaceful & private. My daughter was privileged to be in your home about ten years ago when you & your husband were thanking some of the Labour party's loyal supporters & voluntary workers. I myself am a retired infant Teacher & have voted Labour for many years & my Tribute to your wonderful husband will be to take out full memberships in his beloved Labour party, to which he gave his all.

Yours respectfully

Margaret Jackson

Replied
July

DR JOHN CHISHOLM
30 Crisp Road
Henley-on-Thames, Oxon, RG9 2EP
—
Telephone 0491-575343
Fax 0491-572413

17 V 94

Dear Mrs Smith

I am writing to you because I like countless others have been grieving and shedding tears after the death of your husband. He was a shining example of honesty, integrity, compassion, and a fierce determination to achieve equity and fairness and to strive to eliminate poverty in British society. Politics would again be seen as the high and honourable calling it is if it contained more men like John Smith.

I have been moved by the humanity and sincerity of the tributes which have been paid by politicians of all parties, but particularly by Tony Benn's description of 'a lovely man' who would express the same, consistent views in any setting, and by Neil Kinnock's anger that your husband was denied the chance to show the full scope of his great talents in the highest office. Never since Hugh Gaitskell's death has Britain been so cruelly denied the leadership it needs.

You and your daughters will now be overwhelmed by grief, but I hope the realisation that John Smith was held in the highest esteem by so many people, inside and outside politics, is proving of some comfort to you.

Yours sincerely

John Chisholm

14. 5. 94.

Replied
July

SGT S. IRVING
WO's & SGT's MESS
27 TPT REGT RLC
BULLER BRKS
ALDERSHOT
HANTS GU11 2BX

Dear Sir,

I'm not a Labour party member, and there are few politician whose passing I would mourn. The news of John Smith's death was enough to reduce me to tears; his untimely and tragic departure has denied us the chance of a Great Prime Minister, but at least we can keep the memory of a Great Man.

I don't know whether or not it will be possible to forward the enclosed card to Mrs. Smith, but sending the card was the least I could do in the hope that sharing grief might lessen the burden.

With deepest sympathy,
Scott Irving

THE RELIGIOUS SOCIETY OF FRIENDS (QUAKERS)

SOUTH EAST SCOTLAND MONTHLY MEETING

Replied august

Quaker Meeting House
7 Victoria Terrace
Edinburgh EH1 2JL

Please reply to: 14 Ethel Terrace,
Flat 36
Edinburgh EH10 5NA
031-447-4957

Tel. 031-225 4825

25th May, 1994

Dear Elisabeth Smith,

The members of the Quaker Community in the South East of Scotland have asked me to convey to you and your daughters our sympathy at this time of great sadness in your family. It was with very deep distress that we heard of the death of your husband, for we have watched with growing admiration the influence on the Labour Party, and far beyond, of his wisdom, and his understanding of the deepest needs of the great variety of the individuals and the communities which form our country.

We are confident that his vision, and his integrity in all that he thought and did, will continue to enrich the lives not only of many of our policy makers, but also of those 'ordinary' people who have been inspired by his example to do what they can to combat injustice and despair.

Yours sincerely,

Jenny Neilson

(Jenny Neilson - Clerk to South East Scotland Monthly Meeting)

Please do not trouble to reply to this note.

Replied July

The British Council

Promoting cultural, educational
and technical co-operation between
Britain and other countries

MRS ELIZABETH SMITH
21 Cluny Drive
Morningside
Edinburgh EH10 6AW
Scotland

No.7 3rd Street, New Manila
Quezon City, Metro Manila
Telephone 7211981/2/3/4
Telex 63199 ETPIMO PN

20 May 1994

Dear Elizabeth,

I write, from the other side of the world, to say how
stunned and saddened we were to read of John's death, and
to send you and your daughters our heartfelt condolences.

The personal loss to you and the family is private, and
incalculable. The loss to the nation is public, and equally
incalculable, for in an age of political cyncicism, and low
standards in high places, John, with his Scottish
Presbyterian background, his concern for the people, his
contempt for economic theories that accept the
inevitability and sheer waste of long-term, mass
unemployment, his intellect, integrity, humour, and warm
human sympathy, John was a beacon of hope for a country in
travail.

He was, I believe, the best hope for a misgoverned and
increasingly disillusioned Britain, desperate for
leadership, and the restoration of some of the old
certainties and decencies. Whatever deep concern we have
felt about our country over recent years is sharpened,
rendered more acute and poignant, by his death. Your
personal grief is shared by millions, who looked to him as
tomorrow's leader, and his untimely passing is a profound
national tragedy for Britain at this ebb-tide in its
history.

May he rest in peace, on Iona, with the ancient kings of
Scotland.

To you and the girls we send our deepest sympathy for your
personal loss, and our best wishes during these dark and
diffciult days.

Yours sincerely,

Faith and Norman Bissett

UNION OF COMMUNICATION WORKERS

General Secretary: Alan Johnson
U.C.W. HOUSE CRESCENT LANE LONDON SW4 9RN
Telephone: 071-622 9977

Elizabeth Smith
21 Cluny Drive
Edinburgh
EH10 6DW

13th May 1994

Dear Elizabeth,

We have been devastated by John's death. We had personal experience of his warmth and kindness but we write to express the sorrow and grief of all the members that we represent. Postal and telecommunication workers, regardless of their political preference, viewed John as a man of commanding intregity and a politician who was more concerned with ethics than point scoring.

John was due to speak at our 75th Annual Conference and it was typical of him that he would take the time and trouble during a busy schedule to come to talk to our Conference whose support he knew he would get whether he attended or not.

We were both looking forward to working with John to ensure a Labour victory at the next Election in our capacities of NEC member and General Secretary of an affiliated Union.

We cannot express sufficiently the sorrow and grief we feel, not particularly because we have lost such a good Leader but because we have lost such a lovely man. The thoughts of everyone in the

- 2 -

Union is with you and your daughters who gave such wonderful support and have been left so cruelly deprived.

John lived and probably died for the Labour movement and its commitment to peace and social justice.

Yours in deepest sympathy

ALAN JOHNSON
General Secretary

DEREK HODGSON
Deputy General Secretary

205

Replied
June

9, West Row,
Greatham,
Hartlepool,
Cleveland,
TS25 2HW.
27th May 1994.

Dear Mrs. Smith,

When I heard of the death of your husband on Thursday 12th of May I felt
so sad that I cried - I can't imagine this happening with any other
politician.
Although I only knew of John Smith through the media, and then only for
the short time since he became leader of the Labour Party, I felt as though
I had suffered a personal loss.   Reactions from the public show that many
other people feel the same.

I am deeply sorry that we have lost from public life a man with such
integrity, humanity, compassion, intelligence, wit and humour. Above all
he demonstrated the strength that comes from a loving and united family,
how delightful it was to see this.

" A crane calling in the shade.
  Its young answers it.
  I have a good goblet.
  I will share it with you.

This refers to the involuntary influence of a man's inner being upon
persons of a kindred spirit. The crane need not show itself on a high hill.
It may be quite hidden when it sounds its call; yet its young will hear its
note, will recognize it and give answer. Where there is a joyous mood,
there a comrade will appear to share a glass of wine.
This is the echo awakened in men through spiritual attraction. Whenever
a feeling is voiced with truth and frankness, whenever a deed is the clear
expression of sentiment, a mysterious and far-reaching influence is exerted.
At first it acts on those who are inwardly receptive. But the circle grows
larger and larger. The root of all influence lies in one's own inner being:
given true and vigorous expression in word and deed its effect is great.
The effect is but the reflection of something that emanates from one's
own heart."
Verse from Inner Truth, I Ching.

My deepest sympathy goes to you and your daughters for the loss of a man
who was so obviously an adorable husband and father. The loss to us all
is profound.

Yours sincerely,

Mrs. S.C.Plows.